THE HEART'S HANDBOOK:

16 LESSONS ON LOVE

DR. TRIVENI SHARMA

Powered by

24by7Publishing.com

This book **"The Heart's Handbook: 16 Lessons on Love"** by Dr. Triveni Sharma is self-published by the author.

All the printing & distribution processes of the book is powered by

24by7 Publishing
13 New Road, Kolkata - 51, India
https://www.24by7Publishing.com
mail@24by7publishing.com
+91 9831 470 133
+91 9433 444 334

MRP: INR 349.00

First Published in September, 2024

Version 1.00

ISBN: 978-81-972447-2-8

Powered by

24by7Publishing.com

Love has been a part of our lives, whether it has been reciprocated in romantic relationships or not, that is a different story. Romance excites everyone. It is beautiful being in love and experiencing romantic relationships. For centuries poets, cinema, music and art have been portraying love and romance in different perspectives. Philosophy that is lovingly referred to as the mother of psychology has also been discovering the emotion of love and expressions of romance since ages. Psychology in the contemporary world has tried decoding romantic relationships a bit differently. The good side and the ugly side of romantic relationships seems a bit rational if we understand what all goes into this simple emotion called love and a really fancy desirable expression called romance. This book will take you through different aspects of romantic relationships and you might turn out to be a better lover who has just been psychologically groomed to understand romance better.

Dedicated to all the lovers.

INDEX

CHAPTER – 1

What is Love?

It was in the fourth standard that Rishika saw a new boy entering their class; she looked at him and felt something different. Talking to him in the class started being her high point thereafter. Of course, a few months down the line she started asking herself, whether happening to her. Years later, she liked someone again, and she started getting intrigued with the distinction between "love" and some fancy word she heard on the TV "infatuation". So, all of us somewhere started analyzing our feelings and got interested in the phenomenon called "Love". Although today, there are zillion other scenarios that have made the concept of love a bit complex.

Since this is a book largely based on psychology, let's look at love through the science that understands humans and emotions.

Philosophers tried understanding love as well and Henry Finck(1902) remarked " Love is such a tissue of paradoxes and exists in such an endless varieties of forms and shades that you may say anything about it that you please and it is likely to be correct".

Finck seems to be right. Love is subjective. For some it can be understanding and compatibility whereas for some it can be a way to laugh and hustle together, whereas for some it can be related to loyalty. There are as many definitions of love as thereare lovers.

Sigmund Freud is the most famous psychologists outside psychology and he defined love in this characteristic way as "the desire of sexual union at the core of emotion." Although he added that when that desire of sexual impulse is defeated, people compensate for the frustration by painting a rosy picture of another person and romanticizing falling in love with him or her.

Another Psychologist Fromm in 1956 defined love as a device that is used to reduce loneliness and isolation. Harlow in 1958 defined love as a wondrous state that is deep, tender and rewarding.

So, if we try to derive an inference from the definitions we can refer to what American Psychological Association defines love in contemporary world as a "complex" emotion that involves: Affection toward another individual, a sense of tenderness, sensitivity to their responses, experiencing pleasure due to another individual.

What is Romance?

Love is beautiful because it has romance. One of the fundamental feelings that result from love is romance. It is an exciting, wandering, delightful, gentle, and fulfilling condition. Books, periodicals, and films have all been centered on this thrilling subject. Every language has its own words and descriptions for love, such as in Greek love is calledagape, in Sanskrit love is Prema, in Swahili it is Upenda, in Arabic it is Rahman and so on.

A romantic relationship is marked by unique displays of affection and closeness between two people and is reciprocal, continuing and voluntary (Collins, et al., 2009). Our interactions have an impact on our identity, opportunity, and behaviours. Understanding relationships is essential since they play such a significant part in our lives. The beginning, middle, and end of a relationship, as well as how these three stages of a relationship change through time, all have an impact on how we feel about ourselves and other people. There has been a lot of research on friendships and relationships in general but there hasn't been as much done on romantic relationships and the psychological variables that underlie them. Understanding these romantic relationships is crucial because they can have a huge effect on our lives and romantic relationships are ones in which we invest a lot of time and energy. Romantic relationships start to affect our life since we areteenagers. Because romance is so prevalent in our culture, we admire it (Settersten 2015).

Science of Love

Here we explore various theories that try to explain the mystery of love. One of the most fascinating and enigmatic topics of human kind is love, an emotion that has served as the inspiration for innumerable pieces of philosophy, literature, and art. This chapter offers a thorough overview, covering everything from psychological frameworks that break down love into its constituent parts—such as closeness, passion and commitment—to sociological views that see love through the lens of social structures and cultural norms.

Evolutionary Approach

According to this theory living beings are motivated by an instinct for survival of the fittest and they search for a mate that can help them in the propagation of their species. Anisogamy describes how males and femalesuse different strategies in choosing their romantic interests. Females value quality over quantity. They find partners who are more resourceful, genetically fit and have a willingness to provide maximum to the females and children. Males on the other hand prefer quantity over quality. For males, the target is to have as many partners as possible and for this goal they compete with other males.

The rich array of adaptations and byproducts that make up romantic love serve a variety of reproductive functions. Love is nearly a universal principle (Buss, 2019) and is characterized by a range of cognitive, emotional, behavioural, social, genetic, neural, and endocrine activity. It affects both sexes equally throughout the lifespan. Depending on the life stage and length, romantic love can have a range of purposes, such as mate selection, courtship, sex, and pair-bonding.

Hierarchy of Needs Theory

Maslow (1908- 1970) described that each one of us has the tendency to work for needs in a hierarchical order to reach a final stage called self-actualization. Self-actualization is a stage where one can make full use of one's potential, talents, capacities and the like. The needs start with basic physiological needs which when fulfilled makes an individual strive for safety needs which in turn make a person fulfill his or her need for love and belongingness. Love and belongingness is a desire in an organism for relationships. Finally if all the needs in this hierarchy of needs are satisfied a need for esteem attracts an individual.

The need for self-actualization lies at the top of the pyramid.

The Attachment Theory

This theory was given by Bowlby and he stated that attachment is a set of behaviours that helps an infant attain proximity to a primary caregiver which is usually the mother. The biological dimension of this behaviour is to make an infant stay close to the mother in the most vulnerable stage. This bond with mothers creates a prototype of attachment in the infant's brain which serves as a guiding point for future relationships. Ainsworth & her colleagues (1978, 1982) listed three major attachment patterns in children which are secure, anxious/ ambivalent and avoidant. Cindy Hazan & Phil Shaver (1987) proposed three types of adult romantic relationships based on this theory.

I) Secure- It is being mutually dependent and proximate with the romantic partner. ii) Avoidant- It is being uncomfortable with proximity.iii) Anxious/ Ambivalent- It is practising proximity and dependence but getting a feeling of non-reciprocity.

The Self Expansion Model

Aron & Aron(1997) held a theory that people desire to expand the self and one strategy to expand the self is through close relationships because in close relationships each individual perceives the other to some extent the part of the self. According to this model falling in love is a self expansion activity.

Indian View of Romantic Relationships

Mahabharat, Puranas, Bharatruhari's Shringar Shatak and schools of Indian philosophy (Carvaka, Tantamarga, Shaivmarga, Shaktamarga, Bhaktimarga) hold a very liberal view about love. Atharvaveda has so many rhymes written about love. It is believed that Brahma, who is the Creator, split the purusha into two parts from his divine sword and since then there is a constant urge in one half to find theother half. The Hindu philosopher Vatsayana (3rd century CE) who authored Kama sutra wrote that men and women should marry for love.

Psychoanalytic View of Thought

In psychology, psychoanalysis was the first school to delve deep into the phenomenon of love and romance. Sigmund Freud described love as being derived from instinct. According to Freud, love and sexuality are rooted in infancy (Freud, 1905). He gave psychosexual stages of development and held that an individual goes through five stages of development which includes oral stage, anal stage, phallic stage, latent stage and genital stage. When an individual reaches the phallic stage of psychosexual development boys develop an enhanced love for mothers which he described as Oedipus complex and a parallel complex is felt by girls in which she develops attraction towards father which he termed as Electra complex.

Matching Hypothesis

According to this theory, the age-old theory of opposites attract does not come into play while selecting the spouse.

It's the similarity which initially attracts people towards the opposite gender. Whether it is demographic attributes, personality characteristics, attitudes, values, physical attributes like attractiveness people do seek somebody who are on the similar level like them. During the initial relationship period, when two individuals have not known each other, they assess the extent to which they resemble one another in varied dimensions like values, interests, personality, and other characteristics. The perception of similarity promotes feelings of mutual rapport and positive sentiment between the two, as well as the expectation that further interaction will be rewarding. These feelings, in turn, increase the likelihood that their relationship will continue to develop. The tendency to marry someone who is similar to you is commonly referred to as homogamy or assortment.

Research indicates that both men and women actually prefer the most attractive partner possible. However, although people might ideally want a partner with highly desirable features, they might not possess enough desirable attributes themselves to be able to attract that individual. Because people seek the best possible mate but are constrained by their own assets, the process of romantic partner selection thus inevitably results in the pairing of individuals with similar characteristics.

The Filter Theory

Kerckhoff and Davis (1962) studied couples and found few filters that can explain how people search for their romantic partners. Although they referred these filters to people in short-term relationships. These filters were basically different criterions people apply to find their potential partners. The first filter is social demography, the second is similarity of attitudes and the final one is complimentary of needs.

Soulmate Theory and Work it out Theory

People believing in soulmate theory believe that the current partner is the soulmate, which is found to be essential in their relationship satisfaction. Work it out theorists believe that their partner is less than ideal which was found to be linked to their relationship satisfaction.

The sustenance of relationship stability depends upon the context of living, interaction style, events that happen to people in relationships and their individual characteristics.

Social Exchange Theory

This theory was given by Thibault and Kelly (1959). This theory is one of the "Economic Theories of Relationships. This theory explains the discourse of relationships using rewards and costs. The theorist claims that an individual works to maximiserewards and minimize the cost. The rewards of a relationship include companionship, praise, emotional support, and sex, and the costs of a relationship include stress, time, commitment and compromise. These factors are individual and time subjective, as in what appears to be a huge reward at the beginning of a relationship might turn into a huge cost later and vice- versa.

Thibault and Kelly suggested two levels that determine romantic relationships.

First Level is the Comparison Level (CL) – Individuals

often use comparison level which is their comprehension of their individualistic worth. It depends on past romantic relationships, culture, personality, self-esteem. A relationship is worth pursuing if an individual assesses comparison level is either equal to or greater than the previous romantic relationship.

Second Level is Comparison level for alternatives(CLalt). According to this postulate people will choose a relationship if they find it profitable as compared to other potential alternatives or past romantic relationships.

According to Thibault and Kelly there are three stages of relationships.

i) *Sampling-* in this stage an individual judges rewards and costs of a relationship either directly or vicariously.

ii) *Bargaining-* In this stage an individual exchanges rewards and costs of a romantic relationship and finds the most profitable exchange.

iii) *Commitment-* When rewards increase the costs, which happens once the relationship attains stability, individuals move to the stage of commitment.

Equity Theory of Relationships

Equity theory suggests that individuals experience higher satisfaction from a relationship when there is equal give and take by both partners. Equity is a motivating factor for an individual to stay in a relationship. According to this theory fairness is a concerning dimension for individuals. Fairness can be calculated as one's partner benefit minus their cost which should equal other partner's benefits minus their costs. If an individual has a feeling that one is getting over benefitted or under benefitted from a relationship the perception of the relationship being fair fades away. Anger and resentment builds up in a partner who is giving more to the relationship and the partner getting more benefits than the efforts will experience guilt and shame. If this inequity goes on for a long time in a romantic relationship, the romantic relationship is bound to hit the rock bottom and mark an end. Sprecher(1992) found that females are more disturbed with inequity. They feel more guilt when they receive over benefit and more resentful when they under benefit. According to this theory it is the balance between rewards and costs that determines equity rather than the number of rewards and costs. Equity changes over time and an individual's way to deal with also differs through different stages. This theory suggests that the partner that feels neglected or rewarded will try to regain equilibrium in a relationship.

Investment Model

Rusbult et al. (2001) came up with this investment concept. According to this concept, people will occasionally stay in a relationship even if the benefits outweigh the costs. This theory investigates the elements that may be to blame. The amount of satisfaction, comparison and investment are the factors that keep romantic relationships going. The rewards and costs determine the level of satisfaction. If the benefits outweigh the expense, a high level of satisfaction from a romantic connection is reached; if the contrary is true, a low level of pleasure is achieved and the relationship hits a difficult patch. Second, a person weighs the pros and cons of the various options offered. If they believe there are no better options available to meet their needs, they will prolong the relationship, but if they believe there are, they will end it.

The investment is the most significant aspect of maintaining dedication to the relationship. Both tangible and intangible elements are considered while making an investment. Money, home, car and other tangible assets are looked into whereas intangible factors like happiness, love, belongingness and warmth are also considered. According to this paradigm, there are two types of investments: intrinsic investment and extrinsic investment. Intrinsic investment refers to the money one puts into the romantic relationship directly such as love, self-disclosure, sacrifice, and care whereas extrinsic investment refers to the money you put in indirectly such as children, friends, and shared memories. Rusbult et al. also highlighted maintenance strategies that contribute to romantic relationship stability. These are some of them: *Acceptance-: Willingness to Sacrifice-: Forgiveness-: Positive Illusions-: Ridiculing/ Derogatory Alternatives* -

Sternberg Triangular Theory on Love

Sternberg (1988) gave a triangular theory of love and the theory of love as a story. Triangular theory of love has three aspects –

1) *Intimacy which is the aspect of closeness, connectedness and bond.*
2) *Passion- which is the aspect of physical attraction.*
3) *Decision/ Commitment- which is the aspect of decision that one loves the certain other and in the long term, to one's commitment to maintain that love.*

Relationship satisfaction is characterized by effective conflict management, effective communication, high mutual support, positive behaviour and realistic relationship beliefs. Once intimacy has been established, partners may resolve to stay in the relationship. Although many would agree that all three components are important to a relationship and many romantic relationships do not consist of all three.

There are different types of love according to this theory.

Liking- In this type, there is intimacy or knowledge of the other, as well as a sensation of closeness. Passion and dedication, on the other hand, are not present. Partners are free to be themselves and share intimate information with one another. They may believe that the other person knows them well and can be open and honest with them. These two people are friends.

Infatuation: *This could be Sternberg's interpretation of "love at first sight."* Infatuation is defined as a strong physical attraction to someone. When a person is infatuated, it is difficult for them to think of anything else but the other person. Brief experiences are replayed in one's mind; eating may be difficult, and arousal may be persistent. Infatuation, on the other hand, is rather short-lived, lasting anywhere from a few months to a year or more. It's usually based on chemical attraction and a mental impression of what the other is like.

***Fatuous Love*:** Some people with a strong physical attraction push for commitment early in a relationship. Fatuous love has elements of passion and devotion. There isn't any closeness and the commitment is too soon. Partners rarely take each other seriously or communicate their thoughts. They concentrate on their intense physical desire, although one or both of them contemplate making a long-term commitment. This is sometimes motivated by insecurity and a need to ensure that the other partner is committed to the relationship.

***Empty Love*:** This type of love may be found later in a relationship or in a relationship that was formed to meet needs other than intimacy or passion (money, child rearing, status). Here the partners are committed to staying in the relationship (for the children, because of a religious conviction, or because there are no alternatives perhaps), but do not share ideas or feelings with each other and have no physical attraction for one another.

***Romantic Love*:** Intimacy and passion are components of romantic love but there is no commitment. The partners spend much time with one another and enjoy their closeness but have not made plans to continue 'no matter what'. This may be true because they are not in a position to make such commitments or because they are looking for passion and closeness and are afraid it will die out if they commit to one another and start to focus on other kinds of obligations.

Companionate Love: Intimacy and commitment are the hallmarks of companionate love. Partners love and respect one another, and they are committed to staying together. But their physical attraction may never have been strong or may have just died out. This may be interpreted as 'just the way things are' after so much time together, or there may be a sense of regret and loss. Nevertheless, partners are good friends committed to one another.

Consummate Love: Intimacy, passion, and commitment are present in consummate love. This is often the ideal type of love. The couple share passion; the spark does not die and the closeness stays. They feel like best friends as well as lovers and they are committed to staying together.

Types of Lovers

Lee (1973) offers a theory of love styles or types of lovers derived from an analysis of writings about love through the centuries.

Pragma is a style of love that emphasizes the practical aspects of love. The pragmatic lover considers compatibility and the sensibility of their choice of partners. This lover will be concerned with goals in life, status, family reputation, attitudes about parenting, career issues and other practical concerns.

Mania is a style of love characterised by volatility, insecurity and possessiveness. This lover gets highly upset during arguments or breakups, may have trouble sleeping when in love and feels emotions very intensely.

Agape is an altruistic, selfless type of love. These partners give of themselves without expecting anything in return. Such a lover places the partner's happiness above their own and gets self-sacrificing to benefit the partner.

Eros is an erotic style of loving in which the person feels consumed. Physical chemistry and emotional involvement are important to this type of lover.

Ludus refers to a style of loving that emphasises the game of seduction and fun. Such a lover stays away from commitment and often has several love interests at the same time. This lover does not self-disclose and in fact may prefer to keep the other guessing. This lover can end a relationship easily.

Storge is a style of love that develops slowly over time. It often begins as a friendship and becomes sexual much later. These partners are likely to remain friends even after the breakup.

Hendrick and Hendrick (1986), in light of Lee's description of six different "love styles," offer a description of romantic love. The central core of eros is characterised by strong physical attraction, intense emotional feelings, a favoured physical appearance, and a feeling that the relationship is inevitable. Eros has the ability to "strike" with a quick upheaval of emotion and thought (Hendrick & Hendrick, 2006).

Frames of Relationships

Davidson (1991) suggested three models for frames of relationships.

A **H** **M**

The A-frame relationship is one in which the partners are extremely dependent on each other for survival and are very emotionally associated with one another. The other partner is at risk of 'falling over' if one partner changes. Change is difficult to adapt in this form of relationship and the partners are susceptible if change occurs. A breakup can be quite painful.

The H-frame relationship is one in which individuals' live independent lives. They rarely interact with one another and have different lifestyles. When they do spend time together, it is usually to meet commitments rather than to enjoy intimacy. This form of relationship if it ends, it does not cause significant emotional damage. This frame is a practical sort of relationship.

The M-frame relationship is the ideal sort of relationship. In this pattern of relationship the individual does not compromise their individuality yet they have strong reliance on one another. Couplesfunction efficiently together as well as the individuals function efficiently when alone. Partners feel wounded and grieved if this relationship fails, yet they are still able to hold themselves together. A great sense of self-love is the recipe to achieve this kind of relationship structure. Each person has self-esteem and confidence, both enhance the relationship together and besides the relationship both take care of their own self. Indeed, isn't this the dream of every lover.

Fun Facts

Relationship satisfaction is the highest during the premarital and early years of marriage and declines over fifteen years of marriage for both husband and wife. Attachment security was associated with high marital satisfaction but did not provide a buffer against marital satisfaction over time (Cowan & Cowan, 2009).

The predictors of romantic relationship satisfaction for women are intimacy, passion and commitment whereas commitment does not hold much validation for men

(Rodrigues & Wachelk, 2015). Also it was found that relationship satisfaction in men is determined by one factor that taps into overall happiness in marriage while relationship satisfaction in women is determined by two factors that are overall happiness and the way in which a couple relates to other people including behaviour with family members and friends (Encyclopedia.com , 2019).

Socio demographic factors like physical proximity, societal class, caste, education level and religion also plays a role in your love life. These are basically the factors an individual keeps in mind during the initial meeting. For those who stay nearby, the chances are higher that an individual will meet them and develop a bond. Similarity other factors help an individual to develop mental intimacy. Dating apps and matrimonial apps these days list potential people from nearby areas to choose from for an individual seeking an alliance.

- Similarity of attitudes –According to this rule, those suitors who don't have similar attitudes and values will be filtered out. Kerckhoff and Davis argue that the similarity of attitudes is of central importance to begin a stable and long-lasting relationship. Individuals are attracted to somebody who holds similar views on romance, family, career etc. Byrne (1997) feels that this component of similarity in attitude matters largely in the initial term of the relationship i.e first eighteen months. If individuals find no similarity with each other, the relationships often end in the stage of infancy and do not mature after initial few meetings.
- Complimentary of needs – So, it is said that couples with complementary needs provide mutual satisfaction

to each other which enhances the chances of their relationship to be successful. For example, a person who wants to care for someone and someone who wants to be cared for has complementary needs. It's not so much about opposites attracting, but rather a series of characteristics that fit with each other like pieces of puzzles. Moreover, this also acts as a balancing tool for two people who are trying to live a balanced life. Also, the best part about this situation is that there is no conflict of interest and a certain amount of freshness stays intact in a relationship when the partners are complementary in their needs.

Even if you are trying to ignore love, even then you really cannot escape its presence because love is everywhere and in everything. Humans really desire to discover a loving relationship from a young age. According to Viejo et al., 2015, romantic interactions at a young age are linked to better psychological adjustment and well-being. So, it can be said that creating a huge drama on school romance wasn't really needed. Researchers believe that healthy forms of love, such as the onethat prioritizes the welfare of the partner and the one that prioritizes passion and expression of emotions can prove to be beneficial for our life and can act as a motivating factor in our life.

A study discovered that being involved in romantic relationships is linked to increased well-being. Additionally, it was found that youngsters who were satisfied with the quality of their romantic relationship also expressed greater well-being than those who were not. The simple reason for this is that when life seems to be so stressful and teenagers are simultaneously hitting puberty with a cocktail of hormones display higher indicators of loneliness, body image issues, stress and anxiety. Simultaneously the highest desire to have a romantic connection also surfaces, so if a teenager connects to somebody on similar page they really feel elated and calm. Therefore, a teenager who is datingdisplays signs of improved well-being compared to those who are not dating (Viejo et al, 2015).

Being in a romantic relationship as we get older is the norm in our society. We crave these intense sexual relationships because human beings are sexual in nature and humans want to feel close to other people. It was discovered that the development of one's identity is influenced by romantic interactions that take place throughout times of developmental maturation. It was further observed that links between closeness and well-being are positively related to self-esteem and adversely associated with social anxiety and loneliness. These findings suggest that romance is advantageous to our lives at all ages (Johnson, Kent, and Yale, 2012).

Wholesome relationships are linked to better mental and physical health. If you are happy in your romantic relationship, you will need to see the doctors comparatively less number of times. Your medical bills tend to get shorter, isn't that such an economical benefit of being in love? A person feels mentally relaxed and mental health gets all rosy (Guerrero et al., 2017).

Oh! You might be wondering what romantic relationship satisfaction is psychologically. Romantic relationship satisfaction was defined by the Encyclopedia of Quality of Life &Well-Being research as the "subjective judgment of one's relationship." It explains that relationship pleasure is a subjective sensation rather than an objective concept and that it is unquestionably not a relationship-specific quality. Humans have a deep-seated desire to belong (Baumeister, 2011). But unfortunately, finding the right romantic partner takes a significant amount of time and effort (Fletcher et al., 2015) and once you meet that person, it makes your psyche better(Robles et. al, 2014).Individual differences greatly influence how happy a person will assess their relationship(Dyrenforth et al., 2010).Therefore, it is rightly said - *It is not who you are with, it is who you are.*

Similarly, it was discovered that communication, closeness, commitment, trust, attribution and confidence all contribute to relationship satisfaction. Relationship satisfaction has been connected to a variety of individual and group outcomes, including overall life satisfaction, productivity at work, treatment of physical and mental health issues (Fincham & Beach, 2010).

Romantic relationships are intimate relationships between two people who have a strong emotional connection and are physically attracted to each other. These relationships can take many forms, from casual dating to long-term committed partnerships.

Romantic relationships are built on trust, communication and mutual respect. Both partners must be willing to work together to overcome challenges and build a strong and healthy relationship. Healthy romantic relationships involve open and honest communication, respect, empathy and a willingness to listen to each other's needs and desires. Partners should also be supportive of each other and be able to work through disagreements and conflicts in a respectful manner for the sustenance of the relationship.

It is important to remember that every relationship is unique and what works for one couple may not work for another. However, some common elements of successful romantic relationships include mutual trust and respect, communication, emotional intimacy, physical attraction and a shared vision for the future.

Common Issues in Romantic Relationships

Romantic relationships can face various issues that can negatively affect the relationship if not dealt with effectively. Some common issues that couples face in romantic relationships include:

- **Communication problems:** The importance of communication in relationships cannot be stressed enough. Lack of effective communication can lead to misunderstandings, arguments and frustration. Although constant nagging on whatsapp isn't exactly recommended, healthy communication is vital for a smooth relationship.
- **Trust issues:** Trust is a fundamental element in any relationship and it can be eroded by infidelity, secrecy or dishonesty. Lack of trust often drives an individual crazy in a relationship. Often, even the initiation of trust issues leads a relationship into a deep mess that is difficult to take care of.
- **Different expectations:** If partners have different expectations for the relationship, it can lead to disappointment and dissatisfaction. People should be

very clear with what they seek from a relationship. There is nothing more pleasant than being on the same page with your partner.

- **Conflict resolution:** Disagreements are inevitable in any relationship but how partners handle these conflicts can either strengthen or weaken the relationship. Conflict resolution needs a lot of work on one's own self. You just cannot resolve issues with your partner if you are at war with your own self.
- **Physical and mental attraction:** Physical and mental attraction plays a significant role in romantic relationships. Beauty is subjective, but the smooth sail of the relationship depends on whether you are physically and mentally attracted to your partner. You really need to feel passionate and connected with each other.
- **Personal differences:** Couples with different personalities, values, or interests often end up in a fight on almost every issue. This can cause permanent friction in the relationship. Two people who are already not compatible in the way they see life or two people who have grown apart during the course of their relationship should understand that regular fights aren't romantic and they really need to rethink their compatibility.
- **External factors:** External factors such as stress, work demands, friendships and family issues can also affect romantic relationships. Couples who can work together to manage these external factors are more likely to have a successful relationship.
- **Emotional maturity:** Emotional maturity and stability are essential for healthy relationships. Partners who are

not emotionally mature are unable to understand their partners and maintain a stable and secure relationship.

- **Personal baggage:** Past experiences and emotional baggage can affect romantic relationships. Unresolved emotional issues can cause partners to struggle with trust, communication and intimacy. It is advisable to enter a new relationship light.
- **Intimacy issues:** Physical and emotional intimacy is essential in a romantic relationship. When one partner feels neglected, it can lead to feelings of loneliness and disconnection. Understanding the needs of the partner plays a key role in maintaining a relationship.
- **Financial problems:** Money issues can be a significant source of stress and tension in a relationship. Let's accept this thumb rule- Finance rules relationships, especially *Marriage.*

It's essential for couples to recognize and address these issues early on to prevent them from becoming more significant problems that can damage the relationship.

Effective time management and setting priorities are crucial for maintaining healthy and satisfying romantic relationships. Here are some ways in which time management and priority-setting can affect romantic relationships:

1. **Balance:** Balancing time between work, personal life, and relationships is essential. If one partner is too busy with work and neglects the relationship, it can cause frustration, disappointment, and resentment in the other partner.

2. **Creating a secure environment:** Developing understanding is crucial for creating a safe space for your partner. For breeding physically, mentally, and psychologically a safe space, building trust and creating emotional security is of utmost importance.
3. **Communication:** Clear communication about schedules and expectations is important for avoiding misunderstandings and conflicts. It's important for partners to share their schedules and discuss how they can make time for each other.
4. **Quality time:** Spending quality time together is crucial for maintaining intimacy and connection in a relationship. Setting aside time for date nights, weekend getaways or even just cuddling on the couch or deep meaningful conversation on phonecan help partners feel more connected and happy. The trick is that the partner should feel included.
5. **Priorities:** Setting priorities is also important. If one partner consistently prioritizes work or other activities over the relationship, it can damage the relationship over time. Both partners need to make the relationship a priority and invest time and effort into it.
6. **Stress:** Poor time management and lack of priority-setting can lead to stress and burnout, which can negatively affect the relationship. Partners need to be mindful of their stress levels and introspect whether they are displacing their stress and frustration on their partner.
7. **Self Happiness -** Unpopular opinion, but if you are struggling with the course you didn't want to pursue or struggling with the job you didn't want to join, your

romantic relationship will start getting a jolt. Try focusing on personal happiness before creating happiness in your relationship. *It is a cliché but an empty jar really cannot pour.*

In conclusion, effective time management and setting priorities are essential for maintaining healthy and satisfying romantic relationships. By balancing time, communicating clearly, spending quality time together, setting priorities and managing stress, couples can enjoy a fulfilling and happy relationship.

CHAPTER – 2

Why does Love fade? Are breakup ups planned?

Love, once so bright, can dim like the setting sun, leaving behind the echoes of what used to be.

Love is a roller coaster of emotions. Few people are fortunate enough to experience perennial affection and passion in their romantic relationships, but often, the heavy feeling of fading love and the impending doom of breakup takes over. The initially overwhelming passion and intensity that define the early phases of love frequently give way to the gradual deterioration of routine, unfulfilled expectations and the changing personalities of the people involved. When ignored or taken for granted, the once colourful rainbow of shared aspirations and understanding can begin to fall apart. Love can fade with time, like a beautiful artwork exposed to the weather, as layers of familiarity build up and the vibrant colours of passion become muted.

Examining the various causes of fading love can give light on the complex framework of romantic relationships, which is made up of a finely balanced interplay of expectations, feelings and personal development. This investigation aims to disentangle the nuances of love by providing an overview of the wide variety of variables that may eventually cause the breakdown of a once-shared and treasured bond.

WHAT MAKES THE LOVE FADE AWAY???

Collectively, these factors carve the complex terrain of relationship dynamics, impacting the course of partnerships and occasionally contributing to the love fading away and laying the groundwork for the difficult choice to break up.

Fear of Commitment- This fear is known as gamophobia. The Greek word gamos means marriage is the root of the term gamophobia, which is the fear of marriage or commitment. People who suffer from this phobia are averse to starting relationships; the mere thought of being married or being in a committed relationship makes them feel cautious. Rather, they jump about between casual hookups. (Psychology Today)

It is this phobia that is leading to a declining number of marriages. Millennials and Generation Y are taking longer than ever before to get married. Rise in relationships is an effect of this phobia. There has been an increase in the divorce rates and in general relationship dissolution is rising year by year (Zhang, Y., 2008; Tang, 2005). The relationship literature describes that the declining tendency of people towards commitment leads to breakup (Langlais et al., 2017).

Sexual Incompatibility- Sex plays a huge role in romantic relationships. The complex interaction of emotional, intellectual and physical connections frequently highlights the complexities of romantic relationships. Yet, sexual compatibility is one factor that can have a big impact on how stable a relationship is. The delicate interplay of intimacy, needs and expectations isessential to the general well-being and durability of a relationship.Relationship breakdown and adjustment following a breakup are both predicted by low social reward (i.e., intimacy or meaningful connection to a romantic partner) and high social threat i.e., worries about the partner's negative judgment (Park et al., 2021). If the couple is not sexually compatible, no matter what it will lead to the erosion of a relationship.

The top five reasons for breakup were incompatibility, no feelings left (bored), cheating, a long-distance relationship, and family disapproval (Parija, 2021).

Long Distance Relationships (Physically or emotionally) - A long-distance relationship may be challenging to navigate and requires a careful balancing act between communication, trust and mental resilience. Even with the advancement of technology, a geographical distance can still pose a significant obstacle and cause a multitude of complications that could potentially strain the bonds of strong relationships. A need for concrete intimacy and emotional loneliness can be exacerbated by physical distance. Because there is little insight into one another's everyday lives, trust concerns may arise, which can lead to uncertainty and insecurity.

Couples in long-distance relationships are more likely to separate than those living in close proximity (Krapf, 2018)Long-distance dating relationships (LDDRs) partners if they get closer; they are more likely to break up. Extreme idealization (i.e., idealistic distortion, romantic love, relational reminiscence, perceived agreement) during separation and longer time intervals between in-person meetings indicated instability upon reunion (Stafford & Merolla, 2007).This is the reason why relationships are hard to maintain after a long distance.

Psychological maltreatment of the partner- It includes feelings of anger, jealousy and possessiveness. Jealousy is often referred to as the "green-eyed monster," it has the power to erode even the most powerful connections. Left unchecked it can become a poisonous force that erodes closeness and trust over time. Jealousy might be from a lack of communication, past experiences or insecurities. Conflicts, frustration and anxiety are created in a relationship when partners harbour thoughts of jealousy or distrust.

Research has shown that jealousy is linked with low self-esteem, low self-confidence, low generalised trust, low empathy for others, loneliness, a need for approval, neuroticism, depression, and generalized hostility (Stieger). Research also has linked jealousy with differences in adult romantic attachment style, such that insecurely attached individuals (particularly the anxious insecure type) are more prone to experience jealousy than those with a secure attachment style (Harris, 2009).

Infidelity-Relationship breakdown is frequently the result of infidelity, which is the act of breaking a partner's trust by having romantic or sexual interactions with someone else. It is a very serious and emotionally charged problem. The consequences of adultery are complex and can significantly impact the persons involved as well as the relationship in question.

The individual, the couple, and even their children (if any) experience pain and relationship issues as a result of infidelity. It was discovered to be connected to anxiety, despair, and even PTSD, leading to relationship dissolution (Allen & Atkins, 2012).

A range of psychologically distressing traits, including neuroticism, past history of infidelity, number of sexual partners before marriage, insecure attachment orientation and permissive attitudes towards sex, have been positively correlated with infidelity(De Wall et al.,2011)

Personality plays a role in deciding whether an individual will be oriented towards infidelity or not. Extraversion, high neuroticism, low conscientiousness, and high psychoticism were found to be positively connected with infidelity (Whisman et al., 2007).

Negative self-conscious feelings such as remorse, guilt and self-justification for their behaviour were experienced by the individuals involved in infidelity. Additionally, several unanticipated and advantageous effects of infidelity were observed, such as increased emotional autonomy and improved primary relationships (Salavati & Boon, 2024).

Depriving affection and being inattentive- The person who loves you will soon cease asking for attention if you are not affectionate with them. When one gets rejected repeatedly, they eventually get too shy to ask.

For humans to survive, they must create and maintain social relationships, and communication is essential for this process. As a result, social pain is the result of affection deprivation, which is the state of not getting as much emotional communication as one would like. Additionally, recent studies suggest a significant neural overlap between social and physical pain. Often when an individual experiences social pain due to attention deficit, it manifests as physical pain in the form of headaches, body pain, poor sleep quality etc. (Floyd, 2016).

Lack of Communication Leading to Growing Apart and Losing Interest- One frequent and gradual phenomenon that can lead to the disintegration of romantic relationships is the process of growing apart. People may begin to differ in their courses as a result of changes in their values, interests and life goals. Over time, a couple may lose resonance with the dreams and objectives that first drew them together, leading to emotional distance and separation.

Snooping- A deliberate search for someone's information, especially without their consent, is referred to as snooping (Marques et al., 2016).Snooping is the practice of watching or surveilling someone directly or indirectly in order to gather information about them online or offline, usually without their knowledge (Morrongiello, Hou, & Cox, 2019).The strong correlation between emotional instability, the desire to end a relationship and disagreements is partially mediated by snooping.

IMPLICATION OF BREAKUP

"New beginnings are often disguised as painful endings." - Lao Tzu

The aftermath of a breakup can have profound and far-reaching effects on individuals, encompassing various emotional, psychological and even physical dimensions. The introduction of a breakup initiates a period of adjustment and self-discovery, marked by a range of challenging experiences.

You might have encountered people who have really risen in life after their romantic dissolution and on the other hand you might have seen a few people who have completely lost themselves after their relationship hit the rocks. Several Bollywood films show how one person clears UPSC after a bad breakup and the other one turns into an alcoholic. What determines how an individual will deal with a breakup?

The Blue Sky…

Good things can happen following a breakup, even if it is frequently accompanied by emotional turmoil. Even though ending a relationship can be emotionally taxing, it can also be a catalyst for self-discovery, personal development and a resurgence of independence.

In actuality, "What doesn't kill you makes you stronger." You won't die from the romantic split, but it will come very, very close. It's more like a sluggish, continuous crawl rather than something you can get over instantly. Even though it may be slow, you will eventually become stronger with each inch.You never really know how resilient you are—mentally, emotionally, and physically—until something completely breaks your heart.

Phenomenon called "Post traumatic growth"

According to the American Psychological Association - This type of change that occurs after trauma is explained by post-traumatic growth (PTG). It emerged in the middle of the 1990s by psychologists Richard Tedeschi, PhD, and Lawrence Calhoun, PhD, and it asserts that persons who experience psychological hardship after adversity can frequently experience positive progress.

High Chances that your anxiety can give you some benefit after the Heartbreak!

Anxiety was indirectly linked with greater personal growth through magnified breakup distress, whereas avoidance was indirectly associated with lower personal growth through suppressed breakup distress. It was further found that the positive association of breakup distress with personal growth was accounted for by enhanced reflection and brooding and that anxious individuals' greater personal growth was also explained by their penchant to rebound. Anxious individuals' hyper-activated breakup distress acts as a catalyst for personal growth by promoting the cognitive processing of breakup-related thoughts and emotions. In contrast, avoidant individuals' deactivated distress may inhibit personal growth by suppressing their cognitive processing (Marshall et al., 2013).

Studies have demonstrated that post-breakup, positive emotions can arise, especially if the prior relationship did not allow for personal development and when the breakup leads to personal improvement(Lewandowski & Bizzoco, 2007).

Problem-oriented coping strategies that are focused on emotions and other people, acceptance and positive self-motivation, as well as coping strategies that permit some separation from the stressor, were significant predictors of posttraumatic growth (Zgaga & Avsec, 2012).

Post-Relationship Growth was positively correlated with attachment security, self-esteem, sense of control, growth, perceived agency in the breakup and a cognitive commitment to comprehend and process the dissolution and its implications. It was also positively correlated with acceptance of the breakup, active coping, moving forward or adapting and forgiveness.

Post – Relationship Trauma

People going through a breakup have a complex psychological fabric made up of a wide range of feelings, ideas and coping techniques. The emotional environment becomes turbulent and is characterised by sadness, grief and a deep sense of loss as the threads of connection rip apart. A rollercoaster of emotions from denial and rage to bargaining and deep sadness frequently follows the first shock. The human mind, which is both strong and delicate, struggles with a wave of contradictory emotions as it tries to make sense of the breakup.

Those who have experienced a significantly emotionally shocking romantic dissolution may exhibit symptoms commonly linked to post-traumatic stress disorder (PTSD). Recurrent, bothersome recollections of the relationship or its breakdown, emotional numbness, avoiding situations, people, or things that bring up the past relationship and elevated arousal symptoms such as trouble falling asleep, trouble relaxing or staying focused are some indications of these symptoms (Watt et al., 2023).

Similar to PTSD brought on by other kinds of traumatic experiences, those who have experienced post-relationship trauma may exhibit a variety of symptoms. These can include a persistent sense of hopelessness or unhappiness, trouble establishing new intimate connections, problems with trust, feelings of betrayal or rage and an incessant need to replay or reimagine various events related to the relationship or breakup.

Psychopathology Related to Breakups

Breakups can induce excelling drive in some and it can also

induce excruciating pain in others. But, the less spoken part about the aftermath of romantic relationship dissolution is that it leads to several mental and physical diseases in individuals.

Anxiety, depression, substance abuse, OCD, PTSD, and memory alterations are the mental aspects of the breakup aftermath; besides these, a person can also develop physical health concerns like migraines, skin infections, high blood pressure, increased body inflammation and weaker immune functioning. The loss of a person acts as an arousal modulator and an imbalance in the regulator of stimulation becomes a consequence of romantic breakups that can have various physiological and biochemical impacts. These statistics demonstrate the intricacy of heartache, grief andbreakups (Field, 2011).

People involved in romantic relationships change as a result of the relationships. Together, a couple expands their social circle, hobbies and even self-concepts. As expected, after a breakup, people's self-concepts get ambiguous and their self concept alters. Furthermore, diminished clarity becomes a distinct predictor of emotional discomfort following a separation (Slotter et al., 2010).

Broken Heart Syndrome

Heartbreak or broken heart syndrome is the term used to describe the physical pain in the chest or heart that follows a loss. Other names for this acute pain include "takotsubo cardiomyopathy" and "stress cardiomyopathy". Heartbreak can result in major physical disorders such as cancer, hypertension, heart attacks, as well as weak immune systems and endocrine dysfunction. Even though the pain resembles heart attack symptoms, those who have broken heart syndrome usually recover quickly (Field, 2017).

The impact of the termination of a high quality romantic relationship and a low quality romantic relationship is very different. High quality romantic relationship dissolution on one hand literally makes an individual bed ridden whereas low quality romantic relationships helps an individual gain self perspective, leads to enhancement of self concept and generates elation after the breakup. It often leads to gratitude and higher life satisfaction after the breakup (Lewandowski &Bizzoco, 2007).

Additionally, it has been proposed that there are hugebeneficial impacts on subsequent relationships, i.e. an individual enters new relationships with better clarity of what an individual desires in a relationship and what one can offer in a relationship. As a result, both intrapersonal and interpersonal, the perspective of personal progress after breakup is attained (Tashiro & Frazier, 2003).

Research has found that it is difficult to dissolve a relationship when the couple is cohabiting or has serious future plans. Interestingly, staying in contact with the ex partner also makes it very difficult to move on from the relationship. We might logically think that low-quality relationship will lead to higher life satisfaction after the break up as the dissolution might be the much anticipated relief but quite contrary to this it was found that high-quality relationships make you emotionally stronger and as a result, there is lesser decline in life satisfaction after the breakup (Rhoades et al., 2011).

CHAPTER – 3

Unrequited Love

"I have to admit, an unrequited love is so much better than a real one. I mean, it's perfect... As long as something is never even started, you never have to worry about it ending. It has endless potential."
— Sarah Dessen, *The Truth About Forever* (2004).

You might have felt his kind of love in your life. The kind of love that makes the headache and the poor heartbreak. The kind of love that looks so tempting in movies with sad background music, but in reality really it is not less than some serious life threatening scenario. And how can it be easy? Loving someone with all your soul without getting that love back is not easy. In fact, it is no less than going to a battlefield without any weapon or war gear and getting multiple bullet hits and even after all this, all you can dream about is entering that battlefield once again, thinking you might get lucky this time.

Let's explore One-Sided love or rather unrequited love psychologically.

When a person experiences unrequited love, it can be a complicated and frequently painful emotional experience in which their feelings of affection, desire or love is not reciprocated by the other person. Sadness, disheartenment, body image issues, low self esteem and feeling of rejection are just a few of the rasping feelings that can result from this unequal endearment.

An individual who is profoundly infatuated or in love with someone who does not share the same romantic feelings experiences unrequited love. This can happen in a variety of contexts, including long-term partnerships, friendships, and even romantic crushes. The person feeling unrequited love may feel an intense sensation of longing and yearning for emotional connection and affirmation. It is similar to a situation where you really feel helpless about how you feel.

Unrequited love is love that is not reciprocated and makes one long for a more fulfilling relationship. On a continuum from lower to larger levels of interdependence, five kinds of unrequited love are identified and conceptualized: longing for a former lover, seeking a love object, crushing on someone unavailable and an unequal romantic relationship (Bringle et al., 2013).

Bratslavsky, Baumeister, and Sommer (1998) define unrequited love as "passionate love felt by one person toward another person who does not desire romantic involvement with the [pursuer]". Regan (2000) found that one-sided passionate love is strongly associated with negative outcomes such as jealousy, depression and anxiety. This kind of love can actually make an individual sick.

"Nothing takes the taste out of peanut butter quite like unrequited love"-(Eden, 2010).

Unrequited love has been identified as a mutually unpleasant experience characterised by emotional interdependence and mutual incomprehension. While those who were rejected tend to be more consistently negative in their accounts, would-be lovers looked back with both extremely negative and positive emotions. Would-be lovers, in contrast to rejecters, thought that they had been led on, that the attraction had been mutual and that the rejection had never been expressly stated. Rejecters portrayed themselves as virtuous but nonetheless felt bad about hurting someone; a lot of them also described the would-be lover's constant attempts as bothersome and invasive. Disappointed lovers created stories to re-establish self-esteem, while rejecters created them to lessen guilt. Would-be lovers perceived rejecters as erratic and enigmatic whereas rejecters perceived would-be lovers as self-deceptive and unreasonable(Baumeister et al., 1993).

Personality Types, Attachment Styles and Unrequited Love

There are many different reasons why love is not reciprocated, from personal preferences and aspirations to the plain reality that not everyone will feel the same way about you. Unrequited love can also arise for a variety of reasons including personal circumstances, emotional vulnerability and timing. People who have low self-esteem, high nervous energy have higher chances of falling for someone unattainable.

It was also found out that unrequited love leads to something called disenfranchised grief. This kind of grief arises out of a situation where the loss is not acknowledged by the society or there is a lack of social support for the sadness an individual is feeling, this prolongs the healing of emotional pain arising out of unrequited love. Symptoms of disenfranchised grief includes unexplained headaches, muscle tensions, skin infections, lower immunity, difficulty making decisions, wandering mind, changes in eating and sleeping pattern, feeling of sadness, despair, helplessness and grief.

Baumeister and Wotman (1993)—According to their research findings, inexpressive people are more inclined to read too much into emotional cues and may be more susceptible to experiencing unrequited love.

According to investigators, those who experience unrequited love typically have anxious-ambivalent attachments. Children who had unsettling bond with their mothers act in similar manner with their relationships as an adult. Anxious attachment sufferers are clingy, dependent and low on self-worth. This explains how these individuals become unduly obsessed with someone. In order to show their neediness, this anxious attachment style makes them fall for unrequited love (Davis et al., 2013).

Childhood emotional maltreatment manifested as hostility may result in anxious-ambivalent working which is centered on fear of separation and fear of rejection (Schimmenti & Bifulco, 2015).

According to the development of the early adult romantic relationships model, early family relationships are impressionable for the functioning of adults' romantic relationships (Bryant et al., 2002).

Studies showed that the interactions between parent- child interactions are related to both positive and negative aspects of the emerging adults' romantic relationships (Ha et al., 2019).

ARE YOU IN UNREQUITED LOVE? SIGNS AND SYMPTOMS TO LOOK OUT FOR

It's critical for anyone navigating the complexity of one-sided romantic love to be aware of the apparent indications and symptoms of unrequited love. People who have experienced unrequited love frequently find themselves consumed by thoughts of the person they want to be with all the time, dreaming of a reciprocated relationship that might never manifest. One of the main characteristics is emotional intensity, which can range from extreme euphoria when there is perceived reciprocation to extreme sorrow when rejection or disinterest is experienced.

Signs

1. feeling restless/ anxious
2. dreaming about irrational scenarios
3. firmly believing in self-created hypothesis that the other person might be in love with you or the other person is just not aware about their feelings despite of evidence to the contrary
4. experiencing intense longing or lovesickness even though there isabsence of a relationship
5. initiating contact even after attempts that were ignored or quickly dismissed
6. emotional drain
7. experiencing feelings of jealousy or possessiveness in the absence of a romantic bond
8. ignoring or minimizing certain dimensions of one's life in order to pursue a person who is not interested in you
9. stalking them on social media repeatedly
10. analyzing their behaviourthrough rose-tinted glasses

11. Micro analyzing their conversations or actions to find evidence that supports their own assumptions.

Physical symptoms like altered hunger, disturbed sleep and elevated stress levels might also appear during the battle of unrequited love. People who are in an unrequited romantic relationship may also exhibit symptoms of poor self-esteem and self-doubt, questioning their value and desirability in light of the unrequited affection. An unrequited lover may experience this as an intense fixation on the person, devoting a great deal of time and energy to daydreaming, thinking and scrutinizing every interaction. These emotions are frequently accompanied by a sense of vulnerability and rejection anxiety which heightens the emotional state.

Love is beautiful and blissful but unrequited love can be a misery if one does not handle it. Although there is a possibility of growth that follows unrequited love, if an individual does not stop working on the self.

CHAPTER – 4

Limerence

Limerence is an acute onset of unexpected emotional attachment to a person. Limerence leads to ruminative thinking, free floating anxiety, depression and complete disintegration of the self. Symptoms related to obsessive compulsive disorder, post-traumatic stress disorder, addiction, separation anxiety, depression, dissociative state and maladaptive fantasies are involved.

Limerence was found to be more prevalent in people having low self-esteem, attachment anxiety, weak self-concept, high emotional instability, extreme loneliness, unmet need to belong, validation-seeking orientation, social phobia, anxiety during social interactions and mental wanderings.

Dorothy Tennov first used the term "limerence" in the scientific community in 1979 when her book Love and Limerence: The Experience of Being in Love was published. The book detailed her scientific research on the concept of "being in love." As a result, a disorder exhibiting emotional instability and cognitive preoccupation was identified. Individuals who suffer from limerence (also known as "limerents" according to Tennov) obsess over forging and maintaining romantic relationships with their "limerent object," or LO and have an extreme fear of rejection. Furthermore, the state of limerence is involuntary, conspicuous, perpetual, round the clock and can last two years on an average.

Sternberg (1986), when discussing his triangular theory of love claimed that, "Infatuation is essentially the same as what Tennov (1979) calls 'limerence'".

The essential qualities of limerence are condensed by Tennov:

- intrusive thinking about the limerent object or "LO" which gets way too pushy
- profound yearning for reciprocation
- dependency of mood on limerent object's actions or more accurately, interpretation oflimerent object's actions rationally filtering them according to the probability of reciprocation
- inability to react differently to more than one person at a time (exceptions occur only when limerence is at receding which can be early on or towards the end)
- some fleeting and transient relief from unrequited limerent passion through lucid imagination of behaviour by limerent object that wouldmean reciprocation
- Fear of rejection and sometimes debilitated but always unsettling shyness in a limerent object's presence specifically in the beginning of the meeting and anxiety touches the roof when the meeting is unplanned.
- Intensification of limerence occurs when the individual is stressed or is in adversity.
- acute sensitivity to any act or thought or condition that can be interpreted favourably and an extraordinary ability to devise or invent "reasonable" explanations about howthe neutrality can bein fact a sign of hidden passion in the limerent object

- an aching of the "heart"
- buoyancy (a feeling of walking on air) when reciprocation seems evident
- High intensity of feelings that shadow other concerns of life in the background
- Astonishing ability to emphasize what is truly creditable in thelimerent object and avoiding dwelling on the negative, even to a level that it leads to a response with a compassion for the negative and rendering it emotionally if not perceptually, into another positive.

The genesis and sustenance of limerence is fueled by uncertainty. The person who is experiencing limerence is drawn to a specific "limerent object" but it is unclear if this limerence will be reciprocated. The person ruminates about the limerent object deeply and wants reciprocation more intensely when the situation is more ambiguous (Carswell & Impett, 2021).

People dealing with limerence deal with almost incessant thinking about the limerent object. They might also follow rituals that get in the way of their other duties including constant gawking at the pictures of the limerent object or reading messages from them again and again. Often, the victim plays back to themselves previous exchanges with the limerent object, looking for indications as to what the limerent object might be thinking of them. The limerent individual's mood soars to seventh heaven when the limerent object expresses affection or approval and crashes to despair when the limerent object shows actual or perceived rejection (Wakin & Vo, 2008).

Wakin & Vo expanded on Tennov's research by putting up

a model of limerence that recognised it as a distinct disorder while drawing comparisons to obsessive-compulsive disorder (OCD) and substance use disorder. Because intrusive thoughts and compulsive rituals are present, people with limerence may fit the diagnostic criteria for OCD if their thoughts and rituals significantly limit their ability to function and give them great pain. Wakin and Vo also mentioned that withdrawal symptoms including depression, anger, insomnia, and chest or abdomen pain occur when a person separates from thelimerent object.

According to Tennov, a person may have a limerent episode only once in a lifetime or more often for several different limerent objects. A typical episode lasts between 18 months and 3 years, however they can last anywhere from a few weeks to decades (Tennov, 1998). People of all ages and genders may be impacted by limerence and the limerent object's need not be the same gender as the person to whom the person is attracted sexually, suggesting that limerence is not the same as sexual attraction (Willmott & Bentley, 2014).

Is Limerence Love??

Love and limerence are similar feelings, yet they are not exactly the same. The term "limerence" describes a strong, uncontrollable emotional state in which a person becomes enamoured with another person. It frequently entails heightened emotional responses, a need for reciprocation, and compulsive thinking about the object of affection.

In contrast, love is a diverse, intricate feeling that can take on a multitude of forms. Intense passion and an emphasis on the idealized attributes of the other person define limerence whereas love usually entails a deeper bond that transcends infatuation. Companionship, trust, respect and a dedication to the other person's wellness are all qualities that can be found in a loving relationship.

Limerence is an early, passionate stage of romantic attraction that may or may not develop into a committed, long-lasting relationship. Love is characterised by a more realistic and balanced perspective of the other person and tends to evolve over time. It is noteworthy that although love and limerence are different emotional states yet they can coexist.

In summary, although limerence and love have certain similarities, they are not the same thing. Understanding the differences between limerence and love is crucial for effectively navigating relationships. True love frequently entails a deeper connection that develops over time and limerence is just a strong and thrilling sensation.

CHAPTER – 5

Role of Sex in Romantic Relationships

Let us accept it! Sex plays a pivotal role in romantic relationships. Sex skillfully weaves intimacy between the physical, emotional and relational realms together. Besides the primary function of reproduction, sex is basically an art of communication with the partner that transcends verbal expression and helps to create a special bond between lovers, even beyond its biological purpose of reproduction. The intricacies of sexual intimacy affect people's sense of connection, emotional health and relationship duration. These factors all contribute to the overall resilience and pleasure of romantic partnerships. In order to manage the difficulties of intimacy, promote open communication and develop a happy, healthy bonding between partners, it is crucial to fathom the complex function that sex plays in romantic relationships.

Sex is a defining feature of romantic relationships (Schwartz & Young, 2009)and having a satisfying sexual relationship is strongly predictive of having a satisfying romantic relationship (McNulty et al., 2016).Sex breeds mutual understanding and emotional bonding between partners which contributes to endurance and spark of the relationship.

It was researched that every time an individual gets in between the sheets, the skin shines with a glow of sexual satisfaction and this glow can stay till 48 hoursMeltzer et al., 2017).

Although such ideas are important on an interpersonal and personal level, little is known about the opinions held by men and women regarding the importance of sexual desire in romantic relationships.

Regan's Experiments on Sexual Desire

Experiment 1- If you find your partner sexually desirable, chances are your highs and higher than others and your lows are lesser than others.

Three experiments conducted with students from a university in the Midwestern United States examined both the perceived consequences of sexual desire for romantic relationships and beliefs about the association between sexual desire and romantic love. Men and women believe that dating partners who desire each other sexually are more likely to experience romance and other "positive" interpersonal events in a relationship and less likely to experience "negative" events and stresses of relationship compared to partners who do not desire each other sexually, regardless of how many times they are having sex.

Experiment 2- Sexual desire is equal for couples that kind of like each other and for couples that are head over heels for each other.

Couples who are romantically in love were viewed as more likely to desire each other sexually compared to couples who like one another. Sexual desire was equal in loving and liking relationships - sexual desire did not differentiate these two affective syndromes.

Experiment 3- Sexual desire kind of creates a perception of commitment and infidelity

In couples where there is disequilibrium in sexual libido, the partner with higher libido is perceived to be in love, satisfied, committed, happy and jealous. The partner with a lower libido was viewed as more likely to terminate the relationship, dissatisfied, unhappy and would be infidel.

These results suggest that sexual desire is viewed as an important feature of romantic relationships and its presence or absence in a relationship is believed to have implications for the dynamics of the relationship

As discussed earlier, a key factor in the development of relationships is sexual desire. First, sex is a critical moment in the formation of intense love for most couples since it signifies a fundamental sexual urge that leads to love. Therefore it is said that how a person looks, smells, sounds and carries oneself that adds to the desirability of that person. And the truth is it is easier for people with high sex appeal to choose a partner. Sexual desire and passion are inextricably linked in long-term relationships, so the pleasure and intimacy that come with having sex contribute to the stability and contentment of long relationships (Birnbaum & Reis, 2019).

Romantic relationships have difficulty to sustain when there is little or no sexual desire. According to Sprecher and Cate (2004), a lack of desire might inhibit sexual initiation or receptivity which can result in less frequent sex. This can jeopardize the emotional bond and prevent the couple from the many pleasures of sex including intimacy, excitement, pleasure, healthier physical, mental and emotional state.

Low desire can prevent genital arousal, which can make sex uncomfortable or difficult for men and women. This can result in men and women avoiding sex which can produce conflict and resentment. As a result infidelity, conflict or breakup may result from low or non- existent sexual desire (Blow & Hartnett, 2005).

Sexual relations also strengthen self esteem of a person. Considering the relationship problems associated with low sexual desire, direct declaration and expression of lack of interest in sex can make the partner feel a reduced sense of value and the partner can question the health of their relationship (King et al., 2007).. A decline in sexual desire in one or both partners can cause emotions of rejection, body image issues, inadequacy and relationship dissatisfaction.

Since libido raises a question about the foundation of the relationship, being vocal about low desire may make these worries worse. Couples may be concerned that their lack of desire for sexual activity is a sign of a deeper emotional or physical distance, prospective infidelity, which could cast doubt on the strength and durability of their relationship.

Increased desire for sex might serve as a reassurance to a person regarding the life of emotional and physical bonds prevalent in the relationship. Intimacy-induced passion and intensity can reinforce couples of their desirability and value to one another. Their connection is bolstered by this reassurance, which gives them a sense of acceptance. A sense of reliability in a relationship can be enhanced by an exaggerated sexual desire for one's partner.

Have you heard of a phenomenon called "Compensation Sex"? Compensation sexual acts are done with the tendency to compensate for the cheating that a person is committing in a relationship. Regular sexual acts reduce the chances of doubt that can arise in the primary partner. So, out of fear and guilt sometimes a cheating partner starts mending the primary relationship while committing infidelity. Research on motivated relationship maintenance behaviours demonstrates that relationship-enhancing cognitions support partners' perceptions of the quality of their relationship and contribute to maintaining a sense of comfort and security (Rusbult et al., 2001).

Jong & Reis (2015) found that committed partners are prone to positive illusions of sexual compatibility. Positive sexual illusions, in turn, may foster sexual satisfaction.

Due to earlier experiences such as sexual assault, unplanned pregnancy or childhood learning that having sex is shameful, some people experience anxiety with the feeling of sexual desire or acting on sexual desire (Woo et al., 2012). For these individuals, claiming that they have an absence of sexual desire or lower sexual desire could be a tactic to steer clear of bad connotations with sex.

The attention given to a partner in a relationship can be greatly influenced by hidden sexual desire which is frequently characterised by automatic or subconscious reactions to the sexual appeal of a person. Higher levels of hidden sexual desire have been linked to faster attention disengagement from one's partner for appealing alternatives. People who have a strong implicit sexual desire for their partner are more likely to focus their attention on them, especially when there are enticing alternatives around.

This increased attention to their relationship may help them give up on other possible romantic or sexual interests quickly. Implicit sexual desire may contribute to the phenomena by making the romantic partner more salient and valuable in the person's thoughts. Because of this, people with significant implicit sexual desire may naturally prioritise their partner over other appealing options which cause them to disengage from potential distractions quickly. According to evolutionary theory, sexual desire focuses mental, emotional and material resources on romantic partners in order to keep couples together long enough to raise children(Buss & Schmitt, 1993).

Sexual interest and behaviour in relationships is greatly impacted by attachment style. Securely attached people usually have solid and satisfying sexual interactions whereas in contrast people with insecure attachment patterns may struggle with worry, avoidance or ambivalence which can affect their levels of sexual interest and satisfaction.

People having attachment avoidance experience lower partner-specific desire and higher desire for someone attractive, other than the primary partner. Anxious attachment style did not correlate with someone "other" attractive, but it did predict increased partner-specific desire. Research implies that while avoidant attachment style discomfort with closeness discourages interest in sex with romantic partners, it may increase it with non attachment figures or someone attractive other than the primary partner (Blumenstock, 2024).

So, the worst pairs are where one partner has an anxious attachment style and the other has an avoidant attachment style. An anxious partner will always find solace with the primary partner, and an avoidant partner will get cringed with the attention and will find sexual partners swiping on dating sites or visiting cafes every week.

Having sex makes us confident about our bodies.......!

Our body confidence can be greatly impacted by sexual activity. People frequently feel more pleasurable and attuned during intimate encounters, which can foster emotions of desirability and attractiveness through a positive feedback loop. Partners communicate affirmations of each other's bodies during sex through their physical and emotional connection, which boosts confidence and self-assurance. This is also the reason that people with low self-esteem start dating very early in life and the physical and emotional intimacy often serves as an anchor to them.

During sex, endorphins and other feel-good hormones are released which can improve mood and lower stress levels. This sense of well-being can also affect how we feel about our bodies. These neuro chemical reactions foster sensations of ease, enjoyment and euphoria that in turn supports a more favorable body image.

In addition, the closeness and vulnerability that come with having sex encourages a closer relationship with our own bodies. We grow to appreciate the capabilities and pleasures of our bodies as we experiment with and enjoy physical sensations; this increases our sense of self-acceptance and self-confidence in our appearance.Furthermore, our partners' approval and desire during sexual interactions can operate as potent affirmations of our physical attractiveness (Meltzer, 2020).

CAN ROMANTIC RELATIONSHIPS FUNCTION WITHOUT SEXUAL INTIMACY?

It is possible for romantic relationships to exist without having sex. Despite the fact that having sex is frequently seen as an important part of relationships, there are a number of situations and dynamics in which couples may decide not to have sex either permanently or temporarily.

Ultimately, rather than sexual proximity, the basis of a romantic relationship is the emotional bond and respect shared between partners. Although having sex can strengthen a couple's bond, it is not necessary for a loving and satisfying relationship.

Recently there has been an upsurge in the trend of friendship marriages. In such kind of associations the friends make a pact of sharing life and space with each other, but there is agreement on no sexual relations. Often, there is a club that believes in the theory that sexual interactions often bitter the sweetness of love which is the primary ingredient of any friendship. Some people believe that it is easier and relaxing to maintain friendships rather than engagement in sexual relationships.

A very famous line from a bollywood movie reaffirms this concept "Pyaar meinjunoon hai, par dosti mein sukoon hai".

CHAPTER – 6

Sexting

The term "sexting," comes from the words "sex" and "texting," describes the practice of sending sexually suggestive texts, images or videos using messaging apps, social media or other electronic communication platforms. This is more common today than ever, particularly with the growing use of cell phones and other digital communication tools. We have seen a generation obsessing about love letters, where letters written with poetic expressions, words written sometimes with blood to show affection, letters that smelled like roses and occasionally had droplets of tears measuring the pain of distance in the lovers heart.

But now there is something that kind of tries to imitate the same emotion. In this time and age, sexting has proved to be a measure of love for their partner, and in some cases, it is a measure of outright lust that gets one to attain satiety by touching oneself while looking at the sexts(sexual texts), which might not necessarily have been sent by the partner.

The terrain of intimate relationships, sexual expression and interpersonal communication has altered dramatically since the advent of sexting. Regardless of physical intimacy, it gives people a way to explore their sexuality, have sensual interactions and keep relationships with benefits that go with their fast paced, sort of stressful life. Furthermore, sexting allows people to express and experiment with their sexuality by flirting and sharing fantasies, wants and seductive messages with their partners or with some random online friend or in some online adult room.

Numerous studies concentrate on the consequences of sexting, especially the negative outcomes (Benotsch et al., 2013) such as substance abuse, sextortion, bullying, development of anxiety, depression, low self esteem, loss of self respect and other sexually risky behaviour. But there is also evidence that sexting is linked to favourable outcomes in relationships such as sexual exploration and maintaining relationship happiness (Drouin et al., 2017). There is growing evidence that adults, especially those in committed relationships may benefit from sexting in terms of relationship satisfaction (Stasko & Geller, 2015). Sexting can boost self confidence initially and can act as a factor that provides trust in a relationship. Although the benefits of sexting were found in the mature population, it is dangerous for teenagers.

According to the research, sexting is also frequently used as an experimental technique and is more prevalent among individuals who are single and seeking a new relationship, (Burkett, 2015). On the other hand, some argue that sexting is more prevalent in intimate, long-term partnerships and can be employed as a tactic to improve both sexual and interpersonal fulfilment (Drouin et al., 2017).

According to Woolard (2011), sexting is frequently seen as appropriate between significant others and studies have shown that sexting with a committed romantic partner has greater beneficial effects than sexting with a casual partner (Drouin et al., 2017).

In the early stages of a relationship, sexting can be a pleasant way for romantic couples to flirt and show interest (Burkett, 2015).

While previous studies have shown that men tend to initiate sexual behaviours with their partners, there is a paucity of research about who tends to initiate sexting behaviour first in a relationship. It was indicated that discordance about sexual behaviour, age and partner objectification predicted who sexted first. Sexting can also work well for long-term relationships (Currin et al., 2020). But according to some research sexting is less common in relationships that are already established (Drouin et al., 2017). It should also be less common in the beginning of a relationship because of the high-risk nature of a sexual disclosure and the lower levels of relational closeness that are associated with this phase of life (Altman & Taylor, 1973; Knapp, 1978). These results point to the middle stages of relationship development as the peak for sexting frequency and is lowest in the earliest stages of relationship development.

SEXTING AND ATTACHMENT STYLES

Sexting is a type of online communication directly related to people's attachment styles, which are social patterns formed at a young age. According to research, attachment types have an impact on people's views and behaviour about sexting as well as how they handle emotional closeness in intimate relationships. According to McDaniel & Drouin (2015), only individuals with a strong avoidance attachment style, a propensity to maintain relational distance from partners—were shown to be more likely to engage in sexually explicit conversation as indicators of relationship satisfaction. Additionally, only women with anxious attachment styles- that is, those who crave emotional connection and may experience anxiety about leaving a partner—were linked to relationship satisfaction when it came to sending nude or semi-nude images to men.

Particularly in romantic relationships, anxiously attached people are more likely to sext since they always fear that they might upset the other person or things might fall apart.So even if they aren't convinced with sending texts even then they may do so for maintain intimacy and reinforce partner interest (Weisskirch et al., 2017). Findings concerning avoidance attachment and sexting, however, indicate that a higher level of attachment avoidance is linked to a higher frequency of sexting behaviours and may be employed as a tactic to distance oneself from intimate partners (Trub & Starks, 2017).

Sexting is used differently by people having higher attachment avoidance levels according to what suits them. While some use it more to maintain emotional distance and concentrate solely on their sexual relationships, others use sexting less to cut down on communication. People with avoidant attachment often convince their partners how sex is the only part of a relationship that is real and people who are into emotional components are not being true to their own selves.It was also found that sexting is increasingly common and seen as more acceptable as relationships develop (Guest & Denes, 2022).

Sexting can also make conversations interesting and couples engage in fewer fights if they are into sexting. When it came to partnership dynamics, adults who were sexting often reported more commitment and positive interactions than those who were not sexting (Beckmeyer, 2023).

According to Stasko & Geller's (2015), sexting frequency was positively correlated with relationship satisfaction among adults who were not in "very committed" relationships; however there was no significant correlation between sexting frequency and satisfaction for those who were in "very committed" relationships. Therefore, people in very committed relationships like marriage do not sext.

Albury & Crawford (2012) found that couples saw sexting as a means to flirt, be intimate, show affection and signal trust. Sexting can be elucidated as a proof of trust in relationships since it shows a person's readiness to reveal personal and vulnerable parts of themselves to their partner. By sexting, people show that they appreciate and have faith in their partner's judgment, knowing that whatever sexual material they communicate will remain private and not be misused. As a show of mutual understanding and acceptance of each other's thoughts and aspirations, this act of vulnerability enhances the link between couples and promotes a sense of mental intimacy.

Hertlein & Ancheta (2014) also found that because sexting acts as a buffer against shyness and hesitation as compared with face-to-face discussions, it increases communication about sexual themes and reduces anxiety.

Sexting has emerged as the most convenient method of cheating or infidelity. Sexting has allowed people to explore their sexuality outside of committed partnerships without running the danger of getting pregnant, getting caught or catching STIs (Lippman & Campbell, 2014). For other clans that worry about their physical health or feel that having sex goes against their religious convictions, sexting acts as a safer and easier option (Ouytsel et al., 2014).

Sexting offers a secure and consenting platform for people to explore and express their sexuality, which can have a good effect on their self-image and confidence. Through sexting, people can get approval and reinforcement from their partners, which can boost their confidence and reaffirm that they are attractive and desirable. Sharing private messages, images or videos can also make people feel empowered and liberated since they are taking charge of their own sexual expression and desires without worrying about being judged or stigmatized (Barrense-Dias et al., 2017).Many social media platforms like whatsapp and instagram have the option of making an image a one time see. Platforms like snapchat and instagram have an option of notification if someone tries to screenshot the sent image.

Sexting can occasionally be used as a coping mechanism for negative feelings, especially by young people who may not have access to more helpful resources for emotion control. People who are experiencing stress, worry, loneliness or a brutal heartbreak may use sexting as a short-term diversion or escape from their emotional problems. Intimate interactions can give rise to feelings of validation, connection and transitory solace from unpleasant emotions. They can also act as a temporary diversion from emotional discomfort or misery (Morelli et al., 2016).

THE FLIP SIDE ...

Although sexting can seem like a harmless way to communicate online at first, there are a lot of bad consequences to be aware of. Sexting can have a lot of negative effects in addition to the thrill it gives you right away. These include invasions of privacy, emotional distress and negative societal consequences. When private messages, photos or videos are shared online, they can be taken advantage of, altered, or misused, which can lead to serious privacy and trust violations. Furthermore, the psychological cost of sexting is incalculable since people who share private information with others feel anxious, guilty and ashamed. Sexting can also have serious social repercussions since it can damage relationships, ruin reputations and even get people into legal trouble.

The charm of sexting can at first make people feel happy and validated, but as the consequences pile up, people frequently find themselves struggling with elevated anxiety, despair, sleep problems, compulsive sexual behaviour and low self-esteem (Borgogna et al.,2023).

A study was conducted on sexting among university students. According to the findings, individuals who were engaged in sexting had poor self-control, greater levels of stress, anxiety and depression, as well as problematic internet use. Moreover, sexting was predicted by gender, living with parents and regular Internet use (Gómez-García et al.,2020).

Sexting is not always personal. It is not always done with a romantic partner. Sexting also includes the scenario when people upload sexually explicit images or nudes on various sites or pages on social media. Participation in sexting also correlates with the need for popularity (Gewirtz-Meydan et al., 2018). Teenagers who have a greater desire to fit in are more likely to upload pictures of themselves online (Vanden Abeele et al., 2014). They believe that sharing these images of themselves online will help them become more accepted by peers (Baumgartner et al., 2015). Besides, acceptance, exhibitionism which is the tendency to expose oneself and feel sexual excitement as a result can act as a predisposing factor for sexting.

Consensual sexting was not associated with signs of depression or non-suicidal self-harm whereas non-consensual and pressured sexting was positively linked to both of these outcomes (Wachs, et al., 2021).

Four categories of outcomes were identified for sexting: relational (reputational consequences & personal connections with others), behavioural (sexual activity, risk behaviours and perpetration of abuse and harassment), psychological (victimization; sexual abuse/victimization; mental health and quality of life; and emotional outcomes) and systems-level (distribution/public exposure of social media content (Doyle et al., 2021)).

The argument over whether sexting is a liberation tool or a means of objectification is intricate and nuanced and it frequently depends on the viewpoint and circumstances of the individual. Sexting proponents contend that it may be liberating, giving people a forum to openly express their sexuality and claim control over their bodies.

On the other hand, critics claim that sexting contributes to objectification by treating people like inanimate sexual objects who are devoid of compassion and value. They contend that peer pressure and cultural expectations might lead to the commoditisation of sexuality and perpetuate negative stereotypes by putting pressure on people to engage in sexting.

Sexters(individuals who indulge in sexting) showed higher degrees of body shame, comfort with nudity and body surveillance than non-sexters across genders. The findings imply that sexting has created a new sexual space that mixes sexual objectification and empowerment and that it is both liberating and objectifying in terms of sexuality (Liong & Cheng, 2019).

In a nutshell, the topic of sexting is a convoluted component of contemporary communication that necessitates thoughtful analysis and understanding. Consensual sharing can provide a forum for intimate and sexual expression, but the risk of harm from non-consensual sharing emphasises how crucial consent, respect and communication are. It is crucial to carefully negotiate the difficulties of sexting as technology develops and to promote a culture of digital intimacy that values autonomy, privacy and respect for one another.

CHAPTER – 7

Dark Personality and Romantic Relationships

"Oh! You are such a narcissistic person"- Often you hear people saying it to each other in a cool nonchalant manner. All of us are fascinated with the darker side of romance. Well, the proof lies in the list of movies that become blockbusters, novels that become bestsellers and web series that become popular. Let's just accept the fact that we are intrigued by personality types that behave a little differently than others in love. To delve into the shadow side of love let's first understand what a dark personality triad is.

The Dark Triad consists of three overlapping but distinct personality variables: Narcissism, Machiavellianism and Psychopathy.

The complex terrain of romantic relationships frequently reveals a range of personalities and behaviours, some more shadowed than others. This area of study explores the fascinating relationship between dark personality traits and how love, trust and intimacy are shaped. Dark personality traits encompass a range of characteristics such as narcissism, machiavellianism, and psychopathy which are marked by self-centeredness, manipulation and lack of empathy. Understanding how these traits manifest in romantic relationships is pivotal, as they profoundly influence partner selection, communication approaches and overall relationship satisfaction.

Paulhus & Williams (2002) made an effort to define "Devilish" in terms of the "Dark Triad," which is a group of three somewhat crisscrossing overlapping displeasing personality qualities linked to serious injury or the exploitation of others. This triad consists of narcissism (grandiosity, egotism and lack of empathy), psychopathy (antisociality, impulsivity, heartlessness and lack of remorse) and machiavellianism (manipulation, exploitation and self-interest). It is unsurprising that all three of these personalities correlate with a manipulative and cynical interpersonal style, given the overlap of several of their qualities (Jones & Paulhus, 2010).

NARCISSISM

Narcissism is a personality trait characterized by a grandiose sense of self-importance, a constant need for admiration and a lack of empathy for others. Individuals with narcissistic traits often exhibit the following characteristics:

- A grandiose sense of self-importance
- A preoccupation with fantasies of unlimited success, power, brilliance, beauty or ideal love
- A belief that he or she is special and unique and can only be understood by or should associate with, other special or high-status people or institutions
- A need for excessive admiration
- A sense of entitlement
- Interpersonally exploitative behaviour, troubled relationships

- A lack of empathy
- Envy of others or a belief that others are envious of him or her
- A demonstration of arrogant and snobbish behaviour or attitude

Narcissus: Let us join one another.

Echo: Let us join one another.

Narcissus: Hands off! I would rather die than you should have me.

—Bulfinch (1970)

Narcissus was a beautiful young man who rejected all romantic advances, preferring to admire his own reflection. The mountain mermaid Echo fell hopelessly in love with Narcissus, but he cruelly rejected her feelings. As punishment from the Gods for his arrogance, Narcissus was cursed to fall in love with his own reflection in a pool of water.

The conversation above suggests that Narcissus was not pliable to romantic commitment. Rather than establishing a bond with someone as loyal and alluring as Echo, Narcissus persisted in his pursuit of the ideal loving companion. Narcissus eventually fell in love with his own reflection, the only person who could match his demanding standards and the rest is history. The fundamental theory put out by Freud (1914–1957) holds that each individual has a finite amount of love and libido. While non-narcissists direct their affection towards others, narcissists direct their love towards themselves. The inability of narcissists to love others shows up in less loving and more self-serving interpersonal relationships.

Clinicians claim that romantic relationships with narcissists are characterized by a lack of commitment and are shallow and transient. Romantic partnerships are frequently started by narcissists with an exaggerated opinion of their partner (idealization). But this infatuation ends fast, maybe because a better partner is found, maybe because getting a more realistic picture of the other is unwanted and maybe because the narcissist perceives real intimacy or commitment as dangerous or threatening.

Narcissists lack empathy, agreeableness, intimacy and communication. To preserve their sense of self-worth, narcissists are also willing to criticize and degrade their partners. They dislikebeing vulnerable. They often prioritize protecting their own inflated self-image over being truly intimate (Macenczak et al., 2016).

Reduced degrees of commitment are one feature of narcissists' romantic relationships that are described in clinical accounts. It's possible that narcissists aren't entirely content in their romantic partnerships. Narcissists believe they are superior to their romantic partners. This could be the outcome of narcissists with exaggerated perceptions of their own self-worth in comparison to others (Gabriel et al., 1994).

Moreover, narcissists are less likely to be as emotionally invested in their romantic relationships compared to non-narcissists. They tend to remain emotionally unavailable and distant from their partners, often making them feel guilty or apologetic for merely seeking their time and attention. Narcissists have a propensity to gaslight and they are adept at inducing guilt in their partners as a way to control the dynamic.

The combination of minimal emotional investment, emotional unavailability, gaslighting and guilt-tripping tactics creates an unhealthy and imbalanced dynamic that can be detrimental to the non-narcissistic partner's well-being.

According to Emmons (1987), narcissists are egoistic and self-centered. According to Campbell et al. (2002), narcissists also report lower levels of agape or unselfish love in romantic relationships. Thirdly, narcissistic individuals are more likely to perceive and report having a greater number of alternative romantic prospects or potential partners available to them, in contrast to non-narcissistic people. This perception of having abundant choices stems from narcissists' inflated sense of self-importance and desirability.

A narcissistic individual may constantly seek out what they perceive as an upgraded or more advantageous romantic situation. This could manifest as a persistent pursuit of partners deemed more physically attractive or possessing qualities they deem superior to their current companion. They may view relationships in transactional terms, always aiming for what they consider an idealized or elevated "deal." This hypothesis is supported by narcissists' heightened attraction to people with high status rather than compassionate people (Campbell, 1999).

Similarly, narcissists may find it more enjoyable to pursue romantic involvement and consequently, meet new romantic partners than non-narcissists due to their sensation-seeking and game-playing love style (Campbell et al., 2002).

When it comes to relationships, narcissism can have a significant negative impact on them. It can also lead to conflict, mistrust and emotional suffering for both the narcissist and the people around them.

Narcissistic individuals prefer more physically attractive partners and are more satisfied when they obtain attractive partners (Seidman, 2016). They place a higher value on personal traits like intelligence, success and domination than they do on communal traits like morality, warmth, sensitivity and compassion. This is the reason they are okay with cheating. In addition to believing they have high amounts of these liberated traits (Campbell et al., 2002), narcissists also want their romantic partners to have more of these attributes (Seidman, 2016).

You're right, the initial stage of a relationship with a narcissistic partner can often seem like a fairy tale romance. Here's how it unfolds:

In the beginning, the narcissist will put on an incredibly charming act to reel their new partner in. They will shower them with excessive flattery, admiration, and grand romantic gestures. The narcissist wants to create a whirlwind fantasy-like courtship that sweeps their partner off their feet. The love bombing tactics make the new partner feel idealized, adored, and like the most special person in the world to the narcissist. It can feel incredibly intoxicating and magical, like living out a profound romantic fantasy. The narcissist is extremely attentive, affectionate, and may rapidly accelerate the intimacy of the relationship in an intense way. Their partner is made to feel cherished and that they have found their soulmate.

However, this fairy tale is an illusion carefully crafted by the narcissist. Once they have secured their partner's adoration and commitment, the facade inevitably comes crashing down. The narcissist's true colours emerge as the devaluation and manipulation begins.

So while incredibly seductive at first, the narcissist's fairy tale romance is merely an idealization phase used to lure in their next source of narcissistic supply before the toxic reality sets in.

Love Bombing

Love-bombing is defined as the excessive communication that occurs during the initial stages of a romantic partnership with the intention of gaining control and authority over the life of the other person as a way to strengthen one's own narcissistic ego. Love-bombing was found to be adversely related to self-esteem and positively correlated with narcissistic tendencies and insecure attachment styles (lack of trust or value in oneself and others).

Studies on the relationship between narcissism and romantic attraction indicate that narcissists are attracted to those who validate and exhibit reverence and affection, but they are less interested in people who offer emotional connection. The narcissist's need for continual validation of their own perceived superiority is the root of this habit. People who radiate gratitude and adoration for the narcissist are seen favourably because they feed their inflated sense of self and ego.

People having narcissistic tendencies look for a specific kind of partner. One theory is that, given the interpersonal hostility linked to narcissism, narcissistic people may look for meek, docile people who would make better partners—that is, "victims." For example, narcissistic people may find it easier to control and therefore victims often are attractive romantic partners with mood or personality related disorders, family history of conflict or abuse, extreme job stress or some life frustration.

More recent conceptualizations of narcissistic personality disorder emphasize the need to differentiate between its grandiose and vulnerable aspects (Pincus & Lukowitsky, 2010). Those exhibiting grandiose narcissism tend to seek out romantic partners who are similarly self-centered and egocentric. Research shows grandiose narcissists display reduced romantic attraction towards individuals characterized as compassionate, emotionally dependent and oriented towards others' needs. Instead, they are more drawn to potential partners described as admiring, physically attractive and possessing high social status.

In contrast, vulnerable narcissism has been associated with anxiety, depression and maladaptive attachment patterns. These psychological factors linked to the vulnerable expression of narcissism may potentially have detrimental effects on romantic relationships (Miller et al., 2011). Vulnerably narcissistic individuals may struggle to form and maintain healthy intimate bonds due to their emotional disturbances and insecure attachment styles.

The key distinction is that grandiose narcissists actively pursue romantic partners who reinforce their grandiose self-perceptions. In contrast, vulnerable narcissists' relational difficulties likely stem from their internalizing issues like anxiety and depression.

Machiavellianism

The concept of Machiavellianism stems from the political philosophy of Niccolò Machiavelli, offering a nuanced yet controversial view on interpersonal dynamics and leadership. Rooted in the notion that "the ends justify the means," Machiavellianism places a strong emphasis on deception, strategic manoeuvring and a pragmatic approach to achieving goals – often disregarding moral considerations.

Individuals exhibiting Machiavellian traits are typically characterized by their strategic acumen, cunningness and willingness to exploit others for personal gain. They possess a calculating mindset, adeptly employing manipulation and duplicity to further their objectives in relationships and positions of power.

At its core, Machiavellianism embraces a realpolitik perspective, where practical realities and the acquisition of influence take precedence over ethical principles or emotional attachments. Machiavellian personalities are skilled at navigating complex social situations through shrewd tactics, always keeping their self-interests as the ultimate priority.

This philosophical construct, while controversial, highlights the potential for individuals to prioritize expediency and personal advancement over morality and genuine interpersonal connections when striving to attain their aims in life.

In their pioneering study, Christie & Geis (1970) characterized Machiavellians as manipulative, cynical individuals who adopt a capitalistic approach to morality.

According to Bakan's bipolar model of social orientation, Machiavellians are defined by a sense of agency and personal advancement rather than a sense of community and interpersonal connections (Andrew et al., 2008).

Machiavellianism falls into a specific quadrant of Wiggins' interpersonal circumplex model, which comprises the two primary dimensions of dominance and love. This quadrant includes traits such as callousness, characterized by cold-heartedness, self-seeking behaviour and a dominant interpersonal style of being emotionally unstable and anxious in close relationships (Ináncsi et al., (2015; Jones & Paulhus, 2011).

Research on close relationships and Machiavellianism has focused on several facets of interpersonal interactions. Machiavellianism has been associated with a pragmatic love style, characterized by a practical and rational approach to romantic relationships (Jonason & Kavanagh, 2010). Individuals high in machiavellianism tend to exhibit low levels of intimacy and commitment in their relationships (Ali & Chamorro-Premuzic, 2010), as well as mistrust towards their partners (Ináncsi et al., 2015).

Furthermore, Machiavellian traits have been linked to low emotional intelligence (Austin et al., 2007), low empathy (Andrew et al., 2008), fearful and dismissive attachment styles (Ináncsi et al., 2015). These characteristics may contribute to difficulties in forming and maintaining close, emotionally intimate bonds.

In terms of mating preferences, Machiavellianism has been associated with a tendency towards short-term mate choice (Holtzman & Strube, 2013) and an unrestricted sociosexual orientation, indicating a greater willingness to engage in casual sexual relationships (McHoskey, 2001)

Research has shown that individuals with dark personality traits such as Machiavellianism, narcissism, and psychopathy (collectively known as the Dark Triad), actively cultivate positive first impressions. Our findings indicate that the composite of the Dark Triad correlates with effective self-adornment or the ability to construct an appealing outward appearance. This effect was particularly evident for psychopathy when measured independently.

Individuals exhibiting dark personalities seem to possess a knack for crafting appearances that serve as social lures or hooks, potentially facilitating their cunning and manipulative interpersonal strategies (Holtzman & Strube 2013). They may strategically enhance their physical attractiveness, style or charm to create an initially favourable impression, which could aid in drawing others into their sphere of influence.

The capacity to construct alluring facades appears to be a characteristic shared by those high in dark trait dimensions like Machiavellianism, narcissism and psychopathy. This skill allows them to present an inviting exterior that masks their underlying exploitative and self-serving tendencies, at least in initial encounters.

Those scoring high on the Machiavellian personality trait tend to experience difficulties in authentically opening up to others and forming genuine emotional connections. They struggle to align their personal goals with those of a group or romantic partner. Instead, their interactions are often structured in a way that allows them to instrumentalize or use others as mere means to achieve their own selfish objectives (Ináncsi et al., 2016). This emotional detachment and inability to foster authentic closeness stems from the Machiavellian tendency to prioritize ruthless pragmatism over sentimentality. Their interactions are calculated and strategic, driven by a desire for dominance and the acquisition of power or resources, often at the expense of cultivating true intimacy or emotional depth with others.

In their general interpersonal connections, individuals high in Machiavellianism exhibit a dismissing-avoidant attachment style, characterized by a reluctance to form close emotional bonds and a tendency to maintain emotional distance. However, within their intimate, close relationships, this avoidance is further accompanied by elements of attachment anxiety (Ináncsi et al., 2015).The ability to strategically regulate interpersonal distance may be especially crucial in understanding the vulnerability and relational patterns of those exhibiting high levels of Machiavellianism. Their ambivalent attachment style, vacillating between avoidance and anxiety, could facilitate their manipulative interpersonal strategies by allowing them to maintain emotional detachment while also fostering a degree of dependence on their partners.

Individuals with a dismissing-avoidant attachment style exhibit a preference for casual sexual relationships and a sociosexual orientation devoid of emotional closeness (Brennan & Shaver, 1995). These individuals tend to experience less anxiety following the dissolution of a romantic relationship, as they do not truly invest themselves deeply in their partners (Felmlee et al., 1998).

At the core of the dismissing-avoidant orientation lies an erratic faith and mistrust in others (Collins & Read, 1990). They harbour low expectations regarding the availability and dependability of others, believing that one cannot rely on important people during difficult times. This pervasive mistrust leads them to be unwilling to offer or accept help and care, as they are skeptical of others' motives (Collins & Feeney, 2000).

This attachment style is characterized by a paradoxical combination of a desire for casual, uncommitted sexual relationships coupled with a deep-seated mistrust of others' intentions and a reluctance to rely on or become emotionally invested in their partners

Individuals with a dismissing-avoidant attachment style are prone to experiencing negative mood states such as depression, loneliness (Wei et al., 2007), hostile emotions (Kobak & Sceery, 1988) and high levels of neuroticism (Conradi et al., 2006). They tend to experience less frequent positive emotions and more frequent negative emotions (Mikulincer & Nachshon, 1991), with a tendency to more quickly recall negative words compared to positive ones (Baldwin et al., 1993). Dismissing-avoidant individuals often employ less constructive and inflexible emotion regulation strategies (Kobak & Sceery, 1988), resorting to maladaptive coping mechanisms like excessive alcohol consumption (Brennan & Shaver, 1995). This attachment orientation is characterized by a pervasive negativity bias, emotional dysregulation and a propensity for utilizing unhealthy strategies to manage emotional distress, likely stemming from their deep-seated mistrust of others and avoidance of intimacy and vulnerability.

The research found that individuals high in Machiavellianism were more prone to employ negative mate retention strategies, such as engaging in behaviour to induce jealousy or competition within or between sexes. They were also more likely to directly guard and restrict their romantic partners (Brewer & Abell, 2015).

Women scoring higher on Machiavellianism tend to employ subtle, covert strategies to counteract their partner's mate-guarding behaviours, such as being "sneaky" when flirting with other men, a tactic known as covert resistance (Abell & Brewer, 2016). These actions allow them to pursue extra-pair connections while simultaneously preserving their reputation. It is anticipated that the employment of such deceptive strategies will ultimately lead to relationship breakdown. More specifically, highly Machiavellian women may utilize clever methods to initiate breakups in a manner that minimizes conflict and upholds their reputation. Given the tendency for some women to maintain contact with ex-partners as friends or lovers, these tactics may also serve to preserve opportunities for further exploitation and manipulation of their former partner (Mogilski & Welling, 2016). The use of subtle deception and calculated methods appears to be a hallmark of how highly Machiavellian women navigate mate retention, relationship dissolution, and post-breakup dynamics.

Both Machiavellian men and women expressed motives for sexual behaviour that aligned with strategic self-interest, including mate guarding, fulfilling perceived duties or pressures, boosting self-esteem, seeking novel experiences, acquiring resources, elevating social status, enacting retaliation and serving utilitarian goals. Machiavellianism was a strong predictor of intentions to commit infidelity, as well as various forms of sexual dishonesty examined - from overt deception and lying to self-serving rationalizations and avoiding conflict (Brewer & Abell, 2015).

It's crucial to remember that not all adulterers are Machiavellian, and not all infidelity is committed by Machiavellian people. If they do commit adultery, people with Machiavellian tendencies could be more likely to use deceit and manipulation.

Psychopathy

Psychopathy, a complex psychological construct, has long held the attention of both the public and scientific community. This multifaceted concept, which explores the darker aspects of human nature, continues to challenge and fascinate researchers across various fields. Characterized by a specific set of behavioural patterns and personality traits, psychopathy has its foundations in the groundbreaking work of scholars such as Hervey Cleckley and Robert Hare. The study of this phenomenon encompasses several key features, including emotional detachment, empathy deficits, antisocial tendencies, affective instability, lack of remorse and manipulative behaviours. The mysterious nature of psychopathy, along with its significant implications for comprehending human conduct, remains a topic of ongoing scientific investigation and widespread interest.

The confluence of these traits can lead to severe repercussions, affecting both the individual exhibiting psychopathic tendencies and those in their orbit. Individuals with psychopathic characteristics often display a proclivity for impulsive behaviour, showing little concern for the consequences of their actions as long as these yield immediate satisfaction or personal benefit.

Furthermore, individuals with psychopathic traits often show a higher tendency to support and partake in unethical behaviours compared to those without such traits. This increased propensity stems from their reduced moral awareness and indifference to how their actions affect others. Such behavioural tendencies highlight the intricate relationship between psychopathic characteristics and ethical decision-making processes (Ritchie & Forth, 2016).

The term "psychopath" is more prevalent in popular culture and media rather than psychopathy. Interacting with people who exhibit psychopathic traits can have detrimental impacts on one's physical, sexual, emotional and financial well-being (Humeny et al., 2021).

Psychopathy has been identified as a significant risk factor in various egregious acts, ranging from lethal violence (Fox & DeLisi, 2019) to corporate bullying (Boddy, 2011). Notably, it stands out as one of the most prominent risk factors for intimate partner violence (IPV), which encompasses physical, sexual and emotional abuse within close relationships.

A thorough meta-analysis by Robertson and colleagues (2020) demonstrated that psychopathy is among the most consistent indicators of IPV. This finding is especially noteworthy when compared to other well-known risk factors such as aggressive tendencies, antisocial conduct and alcohol consumption. The study emphasizes the strong connection between psychopathic characteristics and the likelihood of violence in intimate relationships. This underscores the crucial need to identify and address these traits in both clinical settings and broader social contexts.

Studies suggest that as an individual's psychopathy score increases, the levels of intimacy, passion and commitment in their relationships tend to decrease. This negative correlation is primarily attributed to the significant empathy deficit that is a hallmark of psychopathy which is essential for emotional connection. Those with high psychopathic traits often find it challenging to genuinely understand and connect with their partners' emotional states, resulting in shallow relationships that lack true closeness.

Furthermore, the self-centered behaviours and manipulative tendencies associated with psychopathy tend to undermine trust and authenticity, weakening the basis for emotional bonds. The emotional world of individuals with psychopathic traits is often characterized by superficial and short-lived feelings, lacking the depth required for lasting, passionate relationships.

Their impulsive nature and inclination towards sensation-seeking may cause them to favor immediate pleasure over long-term dedication. This can lead to a pattern of unstable and brief relationships. Consequently, the combination of these factors often results in relationships that are neither emotionally fulfilling nor enduring for individuals with high levels of psychopathic traits.

The genesis of psychopathy in individuals can be traced, in part, to early childhood experiences. Research suggests that adverse childhood events and maternal deprivation can significantly impact a child's developmental trajectory.

These challenging circumstances often lead to the formation of maladaptive and insecure child-parent attachments during crucial developmental stages.

Irregular attachment patterns can contribute to the formation of maladaptive internal mental frameworks. These frameworks are often marked by widespread distrust, a significant absence of empathy and compromised emotional processing abilities. Research by Kyranides and colleagues (2023) suggests that the presence of these cognitive and emotional irregularities during early developmental stages is associated with a higher probability of psychopathic characteristics manifesting in later life stages. This highlights the potential long-term impact of early relational experiences on personality development and behavioural tendencies.

Research indicates a nuanced relationship between different aspects of psychopathy and emotional functioning. Specifically, primary psychopathic traits were associated with disrupted emotional processing, which is a key component of emotion regulation. In contrast, secondary psychopathic characteristics were correlated with more severe emotional dysregulation (Garofalo et al., 2018).

Further distinctions were observed in emotional experiences. Primary psychopathic traits were linked to greater emotional stability and a diminished capacity for emotional experience, particularly a reduced likelihood of experiencing distress. Secondary psychopathic traits, on the other hand, did not show these associations.

People who exhibit secondary psychopathic traits are linked to high levels of psychopathology, poor emotional control, and amplified emotions as well as maladaptive emotion regulation (Gill & Stickle, 2016). Secondary psychopathic qualities have been linked to attachment anxiety, while avoidant attachment is more common in people with high levels of primary and secondary psychopathic traits (Brewer et al., 2018).

These findings highlight the complex interplay between different facets of psychopathy and emotional processes, suggesting that primary and secondary psychopathic traits may have distinct impacts on an individual's emotional landscape and regulatory abilities.

While attachment theory could potentially offer valuable insights into the interpersonal aspects and origins of psychopathy, the exact relationship between individual differences in general attachment patterns and psychopathy remains ambiguous. However, research has shown some consistent patterns. The boldness dimension of psychopathy was found to have a negative correlation with insecure attachment styles.

Different aspects of psychopathy showed distinct relationships with attachment styles. The behavioural components of psychopathy, which includes disinhibition and antisocial tendencies, were consistently associated with insecure attachment styles, particularly anxious attachment. In contrast, the affective facets of psychopathy, characterized by meanness and callousness, showed a consistent link with avoidant attachment (Christian et al., 2017).

Psychopathic individuals often exhibit a complicated and problematic pattern of infidelity in romantic relationships.

Their distinctive personality traits, including impulsiveness, manipulative behaviours and lack of empathy, significantly influence their propensity for extramarital affairs and betrayal of their partners' trust. Due to their limited capacity for genuine intimacy and emotional connection, psychopaths may view infidelity simply as another means to fulfill their personal desires, disregarding the emotional impact on their relationships.

Their manipulative abilities enable them to navigate dishonest behaviours with relative ease, concealing their transgressions and distorting their partners' perceptions to avoid detection. Moreover, the impulsivity and thrill-seeking tendencies characteristic of psychopathy may drive these individuals to seek novelty and excitement outside their primary relationships, potentially leading to a pattern of recurrent infidelity.

Ultimately, the combination of these personality traits and behaviours makes psychopaths more susceptible to unfaithful conduct. This tendency creates significant challenges in maintaining commitment, intimacy and trust within romantic relationships (Alavi et al., 2018; Sevi et al., 2020). The interplay of these factors underscores the complex nature of psychopathic individuals' approach to fidelity and relationship dynamics.

BREAK UP STRATEGIES -

- Collins and Gillath (2012) identify seven break up strategies: avoidance/withdrawal (e.g. avoiding contact with the partner); positive tone/self-blame (e.g. taking the blame for the break up); open confrontation (e.g.

providing honest explanations for the break up); cost escalation (e.g. making the relationship increasingly unpleasant); manipulation (e.g. hinting to other people that they wish for a break up), distant/mediated communication (e.g. terminating the relationship indirectly); and de-escalation (e.g. suggesting that the break up is temporary). A range of factors may influence the selection of a break up strategy such as the nature of the relationship, personality of the partners which subsequently impacts the partner's reaction.

Research has revealed significant associations between the Dark Triad personality traits and relationship preferences. Overall, individuals scoring high on Dark Triad traits showed a stronger inclination towards short-term relationships and a reduced interest in long-term commitments. Specifically, narcissism was uniquely associated with a preference for one-night stands and friends-with-benefits arrangements. Psychopathy, on the other hand, correlated with a preference for booty call relationships. Both narcissism and psychopathy were negatively associated with preferences for committed romantic partnerships (Jonason et al., 2012).

The Dark Triad, comprising subclinical psychopathy, narcissism and Machiavellianism, has also been linked to communication patterns during conflicts in romantic relationships. Studies indicate that individuals with higher Dark Triad scores tend to engage in more heated and aggressive disputes. Moreover, these personality traits were positively correlated with the use of the "Four Horsemen" in relationship conflicts - contempt, criticism, stonewalling, and defensiveness. These communication patterns are considered predictors of relationship dissolution (Horan et al., 2015).

Research indicates that individuals scoring high on Dark Triad traits are more inclined to use manipulative strategies and less likely to employ compassionate or empathetic methods when ending romantic relationships. Specifically, both psychopathy and Machiavellianism were associated with a reduced tendency for open confrontation and an increased use of cost escalation and manipulation tactics during breakups.

Psychopathy uniquely predicted a greater likelihood of distant or controlled communication and a decreased use of positive tone or self-blame when terminating relationships. Machiavellianism, on the other hand, was linked to increased avoidance/withdrawal behaviours and de-escalation strategies in romantic breakups. Interestingly, narcissism showed a distinct pattern. It was the only Dark Triad trait that predicted a higher likelihood of direct and honest confrontation when ending romantic relationships. These findings, reported by Brewer et al. (2023), highlight the varied approaches to relationship dissolution associated with different Dark Triad traits, underscoring the complex influence of these personality characteristics on interpersonal behaviour in romantic contexts.

Infidelity in a romantic relationship puts both the relationship and the mental health of the romantic partner in danger. Personality differences may predispose individuals to infidelity. Those who have a Dark Triad personality type are more prone to commit infidelity.

Sadism and Dark Triad

Sadism, characterized by the desire to inflict pain or suffering on others, can coexist with Dark Triad traits, amplifying an individual's drive for dominance and control. People exhibiting this combination of traits may exploit others without remorse, viewing them merely as instruments for their own amusement or personal gain. They might employ manipulative tactics to achieve their goals, demonstrating a lack of empathy or concern for others' well-being.

Moreover, the convergence of sadism and Dark Triad traits may manifest in behaviours marked by disregard for social norms and a willingness to engage in harmful acts for personal gratification. This constellation of characteristics points to a complex and potentially dangerous personality profile.

Such individuals may find pleasure in causing distress to others, while simultaneously leveraging the manipulative and self-serving aspects of the Dark Triad. This combination can result in a particularly callous approach to interpersonal relationships, where others' feelings and rights are disregarded in pursuit of personal satisfaction or advantage.

Sadism is potentially more similar to psychopathy and Machiavellianism, than narcissism. It was found that sadism correlated best with psychopathy(Bonfá-Araujo et al.,2022).

Hughes and Samuels (2021) conducted a study exploring the relationships between the Dark Tetrad personality traits (psychopathy, narcissism, Machiavellianism and sadism) and various forms of desired control in romantic relationships.

The types of control examined included control over daily routines, control over independent behaviour and control through surveillance and threats. The research findings revealed that psychopathy and sadism were positive predictors of all forms of desired control in relationships. Narcissism also showed positive correlations with all control types, albeit with smaller effect sizes. Interestingly, the study found that the Dark Tetrad traits functioned similarly in both men and women across all relationship control variables.

To sum up, the examination of the Dark Triad—which includes psychopathy, Machiavellianism and narcissism—in the context of romantic relationships uncovers a complicated and frequently unsettling dynamic. These people may appear charming and attractive at first. However, their deceptive, self-centered and occasionally heartless actions can cause serious relational conflict and emotional pain for their partners. Even though these types of personalities can be quite attractive, especially in the beginning of a relationship, the long-term effects frequently include problems with trust, emotional exploitation and psychological damage. Knowing how the Dark Triad affects romantic relationships emphasizes how crucial it is to develop awareness and resiliency when managing such close relationships.

CHAPTER – 8

Situationship

The word "situationship" has become a catch-all for a type of dynamic in modern relationships that cross the boundaries between dating, commitment and friendship. Situationship frequently lacks the structure and clarity of more formal relationships in contrast to traditional romantic partnerships with well-defined responsibilities and expectations. Rather, they do best in a grey area that is flexible and ambiguous. Without the overt commitment or labels typical of traditional relationships, people might experience intimacy, friendship and even exclusivity in a situationship. As individuals navigate the complexity of emotional attachment without the assurance of long-term commitment, this ambiguity can cause both exhilaration and uncertainty.

When two people have a romantic or sexual connection without the commitment or expectations of a typical relationship, it's known as a situationship. Ambiguity and a lack of mutual understanding regarding the nature and expectations of the relationship are the hallmarks of situationship. They might share characteristics of a conventional romantic relationship, such as spending time together and experiencing emotional attachment, but they frequently lack the

exclusivity and commitment of a committed partnership (Wesche et al., 2018).

"If You Want the milk, Buy the Cow"- A study on Young Black Women

Gibson's 2020 study on young Black women's experiences in situationships revealed that these arrangements exist in a liminal space where Black women often strive to progress into committed relationships to attain the "girlfriend" status. Situationships create an illusion of moving towards committed relationships while actually deviating from traditional committed partnerships.

The research found that situationships tend to benefit men by allowing them to exhibit traits associated with hegemonic masculinity. Conversely, these arrangements often suppress Black women's sexual agency by emphasizing traditional feminine qualities. This dynamic appears to influence how Black women perceive themselves and the dating culture within their community.These findings highlight the complex interplay between gender roles, relationship expectations, and cultural norms in situationships involving young Black women. The study suggests that while situationships may seem like a step towards commitment, they often reinforce traditional gender dynamics that can be limiting for women.

Why Situationship are the "Dark Side of Romance"?

Situationships often represent the "Dark Side of Romance" due to their ambiguous nature and potential for emotional exploitation. These undefined relationships can leave individuals, particularly those seeking commitment, in a state of constant uncertainty and vulnerability. The lack of clear boundaries and expectations can lead to unequal emotional investment, where one party may be hoping for progression while the other enjoys the benefits of a relationship without the responsibilities. This imbalance can result in anxiety, lowered self-esteem and emotional distress. Moreover, situationships can hinder personal growth and prevent individuals from pursuing more fulfilling relationships. The prolonged state of limbo can also lead to missed opportunities for genuine connection and commitment. Additionally, the absence of defined roles can make it challenging to address issues or communicate needs effectively, potentially fostering resentment and disappointment. Ultimately, while situationships may offer temporary companionship or physical intimacy, they often fall short in providing the emotional security, mutual respect and shared future planning that characterizes healthier romantic relationships.

Let us look at these reasons in brief detail-

- **Uncertainty:** Situationship frequently lack clarity about their nature and trajectory. People may continuously wonder where they stand, what the other person wants, and whether the relationship is moving forward or not, which can cause anxiety.
- **Lack of Commitment:** People in Situationship may feel uneasy about their partner's intentions and level of commitment to the relationship because there isn't a clear commitment or set of expectations. Stress and anxiety can be brought on by this lack of certainty about the future.
- **Mixed Signals:** In situationship, there may be times when one partner acts as though they want a serious relationship, while the other partner may withdraw or

behave distantly. Confusion and emotional upheaval brought on by this discrepancy may exacerbate tension and anxiety.

- **Fear of Rejection or Abandonment:** People who disclose their genuine sentiments or wishes to their partner may fear rejection or abandonment since situationship lack clear limits. Their dread of being rejected can lead to tension and anxiety while they work through the intricacies of the relationship.
- **Comparison and Self-Doubt:** In situationship, people could make comparisons between themselves and other people or with romanticized ideas of relationships, which can leave them feeling inadequate or self-conscious. People may feel more stressed and anxious as a result of this comparison because they may start to doubt their own value or desirability.
- **Incapacity to Plan for the Future:** People may struggle to create long-term goals or picture a future with their spouse if they don't have a clear picture of where their relationship is headed. Anxiety and tension related to not knowing what lies ahead might be exacerbated by this lack of focus.
- **Emotional Rollercoaster:** People in a situationship may experience highs and lows as they work through the unpredictability of the relationship. This emotional rollercoaster can worsen stress and anxiety levels and have a negative impact on mental health.

In general, people who struggle with ambiguity, dread and emotional turbulence in their romantic interactions might become anxious and stressed due to the lack of clarity, commitment and stability that situationships bring about.

Who are the people seeking Situationship?

Individuals looking for a situationship frequently have to negotiate the ambiguity that exists between casual dating and committed partnerships. A situationship is distinct from standard romantic arrangements in that it lacks boundaries and designations. People who are drawn to this kind of relationship usually value flexibility and not feeling obligated to meet traditional relationship milestones. People in a situationship, for whatever reason—personal circumstances, past relationships or a need for emotional autonomy—value being able to explore connections freely without the constraints that accompany more formal commitments. The boundaries between friendship, romance and partnership are becoming increasingly hazy in today's dating society, which is reflected in this trend. Secondly, people who are constantly getting disappointed with the recurrent heartbreaks and seek someone emotionally and physically settle for situationship with a partner they like, but since the partner is not ready for a relationship at this point in time, they give in to the demands of the situation. Thirdly people also get into situationship setup as a rebound to channelise the frustration breeding from the past relationship. One – sided lovers who can't get their desired partner often get into situationship to fulfill their needs temporarily. Besides this, committed individuals who aren't happy with their primary relationship find refuge into a more workable setup like a situationship.

Let us look at types of situationship.....

- **Ambiguous Situationships:** These relationships involve romantic connections without clearly defined parameters or boundaries. There's often a lack of clarity regarding expectations, exclusivity, and level of commitment.
- **Fluctuating Situationships:** In these arrangements, partners experience alternating periods of closeness and distance. The relationship is characterized by instability and inconsistency, leading to emotional turbulence and uncertainty.
- **Pragmatic Situationships:** These relationships are primarily based on practical considerations rather than emotional compatibility or chemistry. Partners may engage in these situationships to fulfill social or sexual needs without commitment obligations.
- **Concurrent Situationships:** These involve individuals simultaneously engaging in multiple romantic or sexual relationships without committing exclusively to any single partner. Such arrangements often exhibit polyamorous or non-monogamous characteristics.
- **Idealized Situationship:** Participants romanticize the relationship, often ignoring reality. This can lead to unrealistic expectations or one-sided feelings, resulting in disappointment and disillusionment.
- **Toxic Situationship:** Characterized by harmful dynamics like control, manipulation or emotional abuse. These can cause psychological distress and negative impacts on one or both parties.

- **Dysfunctional Situationship**: Involves behavioural patterns that hinder personal growth and well-being. These relationships often lack trust, effective communication or conflict resolution skills, leading to constant stress and dissatisfaction.
- **Long-Distance Situationship:** Facilitated by technology and affordable travel, these involve partners living far apart with occasional in-person meetings.
- **Rebound Situationship:** Often occurs after a committed relationship ends. Individuals may seek to fill emotional voids, potentially complicating their healing process.
- **Commitment-Phobic Situationship:** Partners avoid committing due to fear of emotional harm, often leading to less open and honest communication.
- **In-Denial Situationship:** Involves mutual attraction without acknowledgment, often due to fear of commitment or rejection.
- **Comfortable Situationship:** Partners understand each other's needs and desires, creating a relaxed dynamic.
- **Physical Situationship:** Focused solely on physical connection without emotional involvement.
- **One-Sided Situationship:** One person desires progression while the other doesn't reciprocate.
- **Passionate Situationship:** Strong mutual feelings exist, but partners are unwilling to formalize the relationship.
- **Friends with Benefits Situationship:** Combines friendship and sexual intimacy, requiring frequent communication.

Knowing the dynamics and kinds of Situationship can help people negotiate them more skillfully, set more defined boundaries and put their emotional well-being and fulfilment first in romantic relationships.Understanding how situationship affects mental health emphasizes how crucial open communication, self-awareness and healthy relationship practices are to developing sincere bonds and emotional fortitude.

Some Benefits

It might look a little bizarre but let us also discuss the brighter side. There are various advantages to being in a situationship that support emotional fulfilment, self-discovery and personal development. First of all, situationship allows people a certain amount of freedom and flexibility in their romantic relationships. People are free to explore their limits, interests and desires at their own speed without the formal restrictions of a committed partnership. Because of its adaptability, people can explore their own interests and selves without feeling obligated to follow established relationship rules. Furthermore, in contrast to committed partnerships, Situationship frequently entails fewer pressure levels and expectations.

As a result, there is a more carefree and easygoing attitude where people may enjoy each other's company without feeling pressured to reach particular goals or live up to social norms. Because there is less pressure, the relationship feels more relaxed and honest, which makes it possible for sincere bonds based on compatibility and shared interests to develop.

Furthermore, Situationship provides a self discovery that supports personal development. People learn about their own desires, communication styles and emotional resilience by negotiating the difficulties of these interactions. They gain the ability to effectively communicate their demands and boundaries, which promotes increased emotional intelligence and self-awareness.

Additionally, without the legal commitment of a typical relationship, situationship can offer companionship and emotional support. Sharing life's lessons, weaknesses and intimate moments strengthens ties and promotes intimacy and understanding.

It can be said that situationships provide a chance for development and progress over time. The relationship may develop into a more committed partnership as people become more aware of their feelings and intentions, or it may lead to people pursuing other interests. Because of their flexibility, relationships can develop and alter naturally in response to the needs and preferences of the people involved.

CHAPTER – 9

Breadcrumbing

When someone flirts or communicates incessantly to maintain someone's interest in a romantic relationship, it's known as breadcrumbing. Another name for breadcrumbing is "Hansel and Gretelling," and it's one of the new, developing ideas associated with the relationship paradigm. This deceptive behaviour occurs when one person does not intend to commit or create a lasting connection. The word "breadcrumbing" comes from the fact that it's similar to leaving a trail of breadcrumbs to lead the other person along. Essentially, it's a method for one person to keep the other person interested and affectionate without putting in a lot of work or emotional sacrifice on their own. This behaviour can take many different forms, such as sending sporadic texts, liking or commenting seldom on posts on social media or making ambiguous promises about plans you have for the future but never following through.

Breadcrumbing can have a substantial psychological impact by leaving the other person feeling bewildered, irritated and emotionally spent. They can doubt the other person's sincerity and the state of the relationship all the time in an effort to get more regular and honest communication from them. In a nutshell, breadcrumbing is a kind of manipulation when one takes advantage of the other's feelings for one's own benefit.

Breadcrumbers don't give up on their calls; instead, they send one odd text or direct message, wink, or post likes on social media sites like Instagram—just enough to keep their recipients interested but not enough to foster a relationship. While breadcrumbing may also happen when a relationship ends, it is not as obvious a dissolution tactic as ghosting because the one who initiates it does not want to let go of their partner. Additionally, it's a tactic for putting a date on "hold" and a type of social dynamic where breadcrumbers are more concerned with staying relevant and appealing to others than they are with being attracted to the other person.

Breadcrumbing functions similarly to addictive behaviours. The main determinant of behaviour, according to the Incentive Theory is the expectation of a reward. Thus, breadcrumbing might have reinforcing effects. It's possible that the anticipation of a potential reward for engaging in these behaviours such as receiving random messages, likes or comments on social media as well as the unpredictability of the reinforcement which makes it difficult to predict when it will be received create tension in those who experience breadcrumbing and as a result, cause detrimental psychological effects.

According to research, those who engage in breadcrumbing, also referred to as "breadcrumbers," have been linked to narcissistic, egocentric personalities, emotional difficulties or problems with self-esteem, as well as a need to draw and hold the attention of others in order to increase their own self-esteem.The people who engage in breadcrumbing usually shy away from awkward or unpleasant situations, including expressing their emotions, due to a fear of commitment. Although this kind of behaviour can occur both online and offline, the most popular means of expressing these risky behaviours are through social networks and applications. Because breadcrumbing is linked to the feelings of guilt, worry and suffering that victims express, it may be a harmful behaviour that is perpetrated over the course of weeks or months (Rodríguez-García et al., 2020).

Are you a breadcrumber?

Just to check that you are on the other side, causing people distress with your breadcrumbing behaviour. Let's look at the checklist-

Manipulative Tendencies: Breadcrumbing may occasionally be used as a tool for manipulation. People who are not totally committed to a relationship may purposefully employ sporadic shows of affection or attention to keep the other person interested. They may feel in control of the interpersonal dynamic as a result of this deception.

Lack of Emotional Availability: When someone refuses to fully commit to a relationship or is emotionally unavailable, breadcrumbing may also take place. They could relish the thrill and excitement of the chase, but they find it difficult to commit to a long-term relationship or to make meaningful emotional relationships.

Narcissism: Breadcrumbing is a common tactic used by narcissists to stay in control and stroke their ego. Their behaviour is defined by a pattern of occasional care and attention intended to satiate their personal desire for affirmation and praise while simultaneously keeping their companion enthralled. A sense of entitlement and superiority is at the heart of narcissistic breadcrumbing. Viewing others as only sources of attention, admiration and validation, narcissists feel they are entitled to special care and devotion. By giving their source(partner) just enough affection to keep them from walking out but never going all in, breadcrumbing enables them to keep control and a sense of power over their partner.

Infidelity: People who are already in a relationship but crave more attention and approval from people outside of their committed partnership are frequently the targets of breadcrumbing. To satiate their personal needs for approval and validation, these people may act flirty or affectionately towards others, showing them affection and attention on occasion.

Breadcrumbing can be used by people who are already in a relationship as a means of addressing fears or emotional holes. Even if they don't intend to pursue a serious relationship outside of their current engagement, they could be driven by a desire for the rush of making new friends and the sensation of being sought after.

Avoidant Attachment: Insecure attachment, both anxious and avoidant were associated with engaging in breadcrumbing. However, there was a stronger association between anxious attachment and breadcrumbing in India (Khattar et al., 2023).

Individuals with anxious-preoccupied attachment styles have a desire for intimacy and trust within relationships, but they might also be afraid of being rejected or abandoned. They are more prone to behave in a breadcrumbing manner in order to stay in contact with their partner without taking on the risk of a complete commitment. In such relationships, those with an avoidant attachment style frequently place a higher value on independence and self-sufficiency than on emotional closeness and vulnerability. To maintain control over the dynamics of the relationship and to keep their distance, they might participate in breadcrumbing. They can keep their lover interested while retaining some emotional distance by means of breadcrumbing.

This can be done by breadcrumbers for a variety of reasons, such as self-validation, ego pleasure or just keeping alternatives open without really committing to a particular relationship. It's critical to identify this behaviour in order to safeguard oneself and keep appropriate limits in romantic relationships.

Do you fall victim to breadcrumbing… Let's Check…

There are few common characteristics of people who might fall victim to breadcrumbing…Let's look at some of them.

Insecure Types - People who are insecure about who they are or whether they are deserving of love and care may hold onto every small or irregular token of affection. People also accept breadcrumbing because they have high hopes for their relationship's future and some people believe that their partner will feel the same way about them in future. In a similar vein, some people don't want to feel bad about not taking a chance or about wanting to treat someone right. And some people find it difficult to set boundaries for themselves, which gives the breadcrumber an opportunity to deceive them.

Insecure attachment, both anxious and avoidant, were associated with engaging in breadcrumbing. However, there was a stronger association between anxious attachment and breadcrumbing in India (Khattar, 2023).

People-pleasers- Individuals who place a higher value on appeasing others than on resolving disagreements may be more tolerant of behaviour that involves compromising in order to avoid conflict or rejection.

People-pleasers are driven by a great need to be accepted and loved by others. To keep the relationship going, they would go above and beyond to meet their partner's wants and ignore warning signs or behavioural discrepancies. Because it provides sporadic reinforcement of affection and attention, breadcrumbing can exacerbate this need for approval, making people-pleasers mistakenly believe that even little displays of affection indicate sincere interest. Furthermore, people-pleasers frequently have difficulty establishing boundaries and making their own demands known. They could worry that talking to their partner about their breadcrumbing behaviour or expressing their displeasure will cause them to be rejected or cause conflict. Because of this, they could take the breadcrumbs that are offered in the hopes that their partner will someday see their value and feel the same way about them.

People-pleasers are more prone to manipulation and abuse in relationships because they may have low self-esteem or a fear of being abandoned. They may think that they aren't deserving of better treatment or that it will be impossible for them to meet another person who will show them love and respect. People-pleasers may cling to an appearance of affection, no matter how sporadic or irregular, out of dread of being alone or unwelcome.

The Soft Kinds- Those who are naturally empathetic, compassionate and optimistic may be more prone to succumbing to breadcrumbing in romantic relationships because of these traits and perspective on human interactions. People who are compassionate and empathetic by nature try to comprehend and feel the feelings and viewpoints of others. They frequently extend the benefit of the doubt to others and could be quick to forgive inconsistent behaviour if they think their love interest is sincere. Because of their sympathetic approach, they may take occasional shows of affection or attention to be sincere expressions of concern and interest, even if the pattern as a whole indicates otherwise.

Those that are optimistic typically have a positive attitude on life and relationships and are constantly hoping for the greatest potential outcome. They could have rose-coloured glasses on and ignore warning signs of inconsistency or disinterest in favor of seeing the possibilities for a meaningful and deep connection during the early stages of dating. This optimism may skew their perception and lead to

The Hopeless Romantics- Hopeless romantics are prone to falling for breadcrumbing because of their idealistic perspective on love and unshakable faith in the prospect of meeting their soulmate. Their deep rooted longing for a happily ever after may cause them to become oblivious to the harsh reality of sporadic and shallow love. Every conversation a hopeless romantic has with a prospective partner is an opportunity to see the production of a magnificent love tale. They make an emotional investment right away, seeing a future full of dedication and enthusiasm. In situations where individuals witness breadcrumbing in the form of erratic texts, irregular dates or vague declarations of future plans, they could cling to the slightest tokens of affection, persuading them that these actions demonstrate true interest.

Because of their tendency to see the best in others, romantics may find themselves justifying their partner's erratic actions. They could explain away their lack of effort or investment by blaming it on other forces or brief setbacks, refusing to accept the fact that they are being held back. Their hope for a happy ending is fueled by their belief that love has the capacity to overcome any difficulties, even in the face of overwhelming evidence to the contrary.

Effect of Breadcrumbing…

When it comes to dating, breadcrumbing can have a big, long-lasting impact on people's emotional health and opinions about companionship. People's confidence and self-esteem can be undermined by the never-ending cycle of hope and disappointment that breadcrumbing creates, making them feel insecure and undeserving of real love and devotion. Furthermore, the vagueness and ambiguity surrounding breadcrumbing can cause people to continuously question their partner's intentions and the direction of their relationship. In extreme cases, the emotional toll of breadcrumbing can lead to depression, anxiety, feeling anger at oneself as well as numbing their emotions, overthinking, frustration,jealousy, self-doubt, self-blaming, loneliness, feeling of emptiness from within, feeling betrayed, body image issuesand feelings of worthlessness.

The cumulative effects of breadcrumbing can erode confidence in oneself and others over time, making it challenging to build happy and healthy relationships in the future. People could become wary and reluctant to make emotional investments out of concern that they might be duped or harmed once more. They may be unable to fully open themselves to possible partners and form the meaningful connections they so desperately want because of this fear of being vulnerable.

Furthermore, people who engage in breadcrumbing may internalize the idea that unreliable and inconsistent behaviour is typical or acceptable, which can create a cycle of destructive relationship habits. They might be drawn to partners who exhibit similar breadcrumbing tendencies, which would only serve to feed their cycle of disappointment and frustration.

The constant rollercoaster of emotions and uncertainty can take a toll on mental health, leading individuals to question their own sanity and judgment. Self-esteem takes a jolt because of the breadcrumbing experience. Some individuals become desperate for relationships while others become silent. The triad of depression includes worthlessness, helplessness and hopelessness. There is evidence of loss of appetite, contributing to psychosomatic factors. People reported experiencing exhaustion, loss of weight, weight gain and a loss of sleep. Besides this there are dermatological effects, as people can also develop redness in the skin and acne for at least 4–5 months.

It may take time and effort to rebuild self-esteem and trust in self and others after experiencing the emotional turmoil of breadcrumbing (Khattar, 2023).

CHAPTER – 10

Ghosting

Ghosting is a contemporary take on avoidant and withdrawal behaviours, usually carried out by cutting romantic partners' electronically mediated ties in an effort to hasten the breakdown of the relationship (Koessler et al., 2019).

Ghosting is when one person suddenly ignores or stops communicating with another person, without telling them why(Kay & Courtice 2022).

The prevalence of ghosting has increased, as reported by both ghosters (i.e., persons who stopped responding) and ghostees (i.e., persons who were 'dumped'). Individuals characterisedby dark triad traits (i.e., psychopathy, Machiavellianism and narcissism) are more likely than others to be ghosters (Daraj et al., 2023).

Ghostees are anxious and Ghosters are avoidant in their attachment styles…

In romantic relationships, both Ghostees and Ghosters often exhibit unique attachment styles that are reflected in their actions and feelings. Those who have experienced ghosting, or 'ghostees', frequently display characteristics linked to anxious attachment types. They could feel more insecure than usual, fearful of being left behind, yearn for intimacy and assurance from their partners. These emotions might become more intense when a partner abruptly disappears, which can cause fear and self-doubt.

On the other hand, people who ghost usually have avoidant attachment patterns. They struggle with closeness, are afraid of being committed and have a propensity to value independence over emotional ties. Ghosters frequently use this tactic to avoid conflict or awkward talks, preferring to put themselves out of any perceived emotional entanglements (Lad & Mansukhani, 2023).

Freedman et al. (2019) explored the association between implicit theories of relationships and ghosting behaviours, intentions and perceptions. They found individuals with stronger destiny beliefs (the idea that relationships are stable and unchanging and that people are either compatible or not) were more likely to have ghosted and been ghosted, more likely to use ghosting in the future and thought less negatively of those who use ghosting to end their relationships.Individuals with higher growth beliefs (the notion that relationships are dynamic and capable of developing and improving over time) reported lower intentions to ghost in the future and believed using ghosting to end long-term relationships was less acceptable than using ghosting to end short-term relationships (Knee,1998).

Ghosting is the Dissolution Disappearance Strategy

Ghosting is a type of avoidance and withdrawal technique of relationship dissolution. Let's look at the break up strategies to understand better-

- Avoidance/*withdrawal* tactics involve increasing distance from and decreasing signals of intimacy to the relationship partner, while in contrast, *open confrontation* tactics involve directly and honestly communicating intentions and feelings with the partner.

- *Manipulation* tactics involve intentionally manipulating or gaslighting the partner in order to facilitate disengagement.
- Use of *positive tone/self-blame* tactics indicate concern for the partner's feelings, concern for their well-being and the tendency for the disengaging partner to take responsibility or blame for the cause of the relationship disengagement.
- *Cost escalation* involves making the partner's life difficult or costly, by initiating disagreements and being generally unpleasant. This strategy involves making it really tough for the partner to keep up with the partner intending disengagement.
- *De-escalation* involves the disengaging partner gradually terminating the relationship rather than ending it immediately and *distant/mediated communication* tactics involve using technologically-mediated methods to signal the relationship is over (e.g., changing relationship status on Facebook, adding pictures with other "friends" hinting at the single status).

Like the assumption that some degree of communication exists during relationship dissolution, the severity of the indirectness of ghosting necessitates a comparison of the breakup tactics that are used prior to ghosting being implemented as a breakup strategy and tactics that are used prior to traditional breakups that end through a direct conversation(Collins & Gillath, 2012).

Ghosting was found to involve less open confrontation, more avoidance/withdrawal and de-escalation tactics. Contrary to previous research, ghosting can occur bilaterally, with partners ghosting each other. Social media unfollowing is an important aspect of ghosting. Relationships ended via ghosting have fewer post-breakup connections than those ended through other strategies. Typically, ghosters initiate social media unfollowing (Collins et al., 2023).

The key findings from a research by Navarro et al. (2021) are:

1. People who have been ghosted (victims) are more likely to ghost others.
2. Those who have ghosted others in the past are more likely to intend to do so again in the future.

These findings suggest a cyclical nature to ghosting behaviour, where being ghosted might lead to ghosting others, which in turn increases the likelihood of ghosting again. This pattern could potentially perpetuate and expand ghosting behaviour within social networks.

Should I text again?

Communication overload (i.e., the feeling of receiving more messages than one can handle) positively predicts ghosting romantic partners.

In romantic relationships, communication overload can overwhelm people and result in "ghosting," where a person abruptly and without reason stops communicating with the other person. The continual connectivity that comes with using texting, social media and messaging applications can put an excessive amount of pressure on people to always be present and responsive in the modern digital age. People may find it difficult to handle the barrage of communications and interactions as a result, which might cause them to resort to avoidance and withdrawal as a coping strategy (Forrai et al., 2023).

In an interesting study on ghosting and dark personality triad few findings were concluded- Those who reported ghosting someone in the past (vs. those who did not) found ghosting to be acceptable and were more Machiavellian and psychopathic. Ghosting was most acceptable in the short-term (vs. long-term) context especially for those who had previously ghosted someone, andthose high in the Dark Triad traits rated ghosting more acceptable to terminate short-term relationships, but not long-term ones.

Research suggests that the acceptance of ghosting short-term partners is linked to certain personality traits, particularly in men. This connection is most pronounced with narcissism and to a lesser extent with psychopathy - both part of the Dark Triad personality traits. The findings indicated that ghosting might be more common among individuals who prefer casual sexual relationships with minimal emotional investment. This behaviour may be a component of the “fast life” approach often associated with Dark Triad characteristics.

These results imply that ghosting could be a strategy employed by those who prioritize short-term connections over long-term commitments, aligning with certain personality types that tend to avoid deep emotional attachments. The study highlighted how personality traits might influence communication patterns and relationship behaviours in the modern dating landscape(Jonason et al., 2021).

Orbiting is identical to ghosting, but the disengager still visibly follows the former partner on social media.

When someone realizes they've been ghosted, they typically go through four distinct stages of emotional and behavioural responses:

1. **Initial Shock:** The first reaction is usually surprise and confusion. The person may struggle to understand what's happening and why.

2. **Emotional Turmoil:** This stage is marked by intense negative emotions. The ghosted individual often experiences anger at the situation, sadness over the loss and may even feel guilt, wondering if they did something wrong.

3. **Attempted Reconciliation:** In this phase, the person might try to re-establish contact or fix the relationship. They may reach out repeatedly or seek explanations for the ghosting.

4. **Final Acceptance:** Eventually, the person comes to terms with the situation. They accept that the relationship has ended and begin to move on.

This progression suggests that ghosting can trigger a complex emotional journey, similar to other forms of relationship dissolution, but with its own unique challenges due to the lack of closure (Pancani e al., 2021).

LeFebvre & Fan (2020) identified two main ways people process the experience of being ghosted:

1. Cautious Communication:

This response involves long-lasting behavioural changes. People become more guarded, especially in romantic situations. They may:

- Struggle to trust new romantic interests
- Maintain emotional distance early in relationships
- Delay pursuing serious commitments
- Take longer to invest emotionally or otherwise in new partners

2. Acceptance:

This response involves adopting a more negative view of dating. Those who accept ghosting as part of modern dating may:

- Become more pessimistic about dating outcomes
- Lower their expectations in romantic pursuits
- View ghosting as a normal, if unpleasant, part of dating

Both responses indicate that ghosting can significantly impact how people approach future romantic interactions, affecting their trust, emotional openness and overall outlook on dating.

The connection between cyber dating abuse and ghosting highlights the complex and potentially harmful dynamics that can emerge in modern digital relationships.Cyber dating abuse encompasses various harmful online behaviours in romantic relationships, including: Direct aggression: This involves explicit hostile actions such as verbal attacks, insults, threats and attempts to humiliate the partner online.Cyber control: This refers to behaviours aimed at monitoring and controlling the partner, such as constantly checking their location or who they're with.

The study found that these abusive behaviours are interconnected with ghosting tactics. Ghosting, in this context, involves strategies like: Suddenly ceasing all communication, using silence as a form of punishment.

Interestingly, the research revealed a gender difference in the use of ghosting. Women were found to be more likely than men to employ these ghosting strategies in their relationships (Biolcati et al., 2022).

Effects

Ghosting hinders psychological and physiological well being (Langlais et al., 2024).

The abrupt and inexplicable end of communication in a romantic relationship, or "ghosting," can have detrimental impacts on a person's physical and mental health. People who experience ghosting may feel bewildered, rejected and emotionally damaged due to its sudden and unexpected nature. Ghosting can psychologically cause emotions of betrayal and abandonment, which can raise tension, anxiety and depressive symptoms. Unresolved issues and a lack of closure can lead to self-doubt and rumination, which can weaken confidence and self-esteem.

Ghosting can physiologically produce stress and emotional upheaval that can show up as a variety of physical symptoms, such as headaches, digestive problems, immune system weakness and insomnia. Over time, persistent activation of the stress response system may have negative effects on general health and well-being and raise the likelihood of developing chronic health issues.

CHAPTER – 11

Mate Retention Behaviour

Mate retention behaviour is an interesting facet of human relationships that involve the various tactics people use to keep their romantic partners faithful and committed. Mate retention behaviour, which ranges from loving gestures to assertive displays of dominance, are the result of a complex interaction between societal norms, individual dynamics and evolutionary drives. Comprehending these actions illuminates the complexities of human mating practices and the mechanisms responsible for maintaining close relationships.

Animals commonly employ the behavioural technique known as "mate guarding," which is mostly displayed by males and aims to preserve physical proximity to a reproductive partner. Male mate guarding has been described as a behavioural adaptation against cuckoldry meant to lower the possible expenses associated with time and resource investments in genetically unrelated kids. However, mate guarding is expected to evolve in females as a response to partner infidelity and the risk of losing partners' resources and protection in species with high levels of parental investment, such as humans (Graham-Kevan & Archer 2009).

Mate retention behaviour or human mate guarding in a more general sense can be categorized according to the costs and benefits that each romantic partner bears and receives (Miner et al. 2009).

The likelihood of employing mate-retention tactics is significantly influenced by the perceived threat from potential rivals. The characteristics of these rivals - including their social and physical dominance, status, attractiveness and seductive behaviour play a crucial role in determining the intensity of mate-guarding responses. In a study by Nascimento and Little (2020), participants indicated their inclination to use mate-retention strategies when faced with rivals possessing various attractive attributes. The results revealed that individuals were more prone to engage in mate-retention behaviours when confronted with rivals who were particularly attractive or displayed seductive behaviour, compared to rivals with other qualities such as high social status or physical dominance.

Buss categorized mate-retention tactics into five distinct groups. Each category represents a different approach to maintaining a romantic partnership, ranging from surveillance to public displays of commitment.

1. Direct Guarding:

This involves actively monitoring and controlling a partner's activities. Examples include:

- Constantly checking on a partner's whereabouts
- Insisting on accompanying the partner everywhere
- Checking the partner's phone or social media accounts
- Asking friends to keep an eye on the partner

2. Intersexual Negative Inducements:

These are tactics aimed at manipulating or criticising the partner to discourage them from leaving. Examples include:

- Threatening to end the relationship if the partner misbehaves
- Pointing out flaws in the partner's appearance or behaviour
- Inducing jealousy by flirting with others
- Emotional manipulation or guilt-tripping

3. Intrasexual Negative Inducements:

These are behaviours intended to deter potential rivals. Examples include:

- Confronting or threatening individuals who show interest in one's partner
- Spreading negative rumors about potential rivals
- Publicly derogating rivals' appearance or character
- Displaying aggression towards same-sex individuals who might be perceived as threats

4. Positive Inducements:

These are actions taken to increase the appeal of the current relationship. Examples include:

- Showing more affection and love
- Giving gifts or compliments
- Improving one's appearance or behaviour
- Increasing sexual activity or trying new things in the bedroom

5. Public Signals of Possession:

These are behaviours that publicly display the exclusivity of the relationship. Examples include:

- Wearing matching clothes or jewellery
- Public displays of affection
- Mentioning the relationship frequently on social media
- Using terms like "we" or "us" frequently in public conversations

These categories encompass a wide range of behaviours, from potentially harmful and controlling actions to more positive relationship-enhancing strategies. It's important to note that while some of these tactics are considered normal and even healthy in moderation, others can be signs of insecurity or even abusive behaviour when taken to extremes.

Miner, Starratt & Shackelford (2009) further categorized Buss's five mate retention strategies into two overarching domains:

1. Cost-Inflicting Domain:

This domain includes:

- Direct Guarding
- Intersexual Negative Inducements
- Intrasexual Negative Inducements

Cost-inflicting behaviours aim to reduce the likelihood of partner infidelity by negatively impacting the partner's self-esteem. These tactics make the partner feel undeserving of the current relationship or any other potential relationship.

By lowering the partner's perceived value or options, these strategies aim to keep the partner in the relationship.

2. Benefit-Provisioning Domain:

This domain includes:

- Positive Inducements
- Public Signals of Possession

Benefit-provisioning behaviours work to prevent partner infidelity by enhancing the partner's satisfaction within the relationship. These strategies focus on making the current relationship more appealing and rewarding for the partner, thereby reducing their desire to seek alternatives.

The key difference between these domains lies in their approach:

- Cost-inflicting tactics operate through negative reinforcement, essentially making the partner feel that they cannot do better elsewhere.

- Benefit-provisioning tactics use positive reinforcement, making the current relationship so satisfying that the partner doesn't want to look elsewhere. It's important to note that while benefit-provisioning strategies generally contribute to healthier relationships, cost-inflicting strategies can be problematic and potentially harmful to both the relationship and the individuals involved. This categorization provides a framework for understanding the underlying motivations and potential impacts of different mate retention strategies. It highlights how some tactics aim to improve the relationship, while others focus on limiting a partner's perceived options.

Materetention behaviours (Buss, Shackelford, & McKibbin, 2008) are organized into fivecategories (Direct Guarding [e.g., "Called to make sure my partner was where they saidthey would be"], Intersexual Negative Inducements [e.g., "Became angry when mypartner flirted toomuch"], Positive Inducements [e.g., "Displayed greater affection for mypartner"], Public Signals of Possession [e.g., "Put my arm around my partner in front ofothers"] and Intrasexual Negative Inducements [e.g., "Stared coldly at a man who waslooking at my partner"]), which comprise two higher order domains of Benefit-Provisioning (i.e., behaviours that reduce the likelihood of partner infidelity by increasing relationship satisfaction) and Cost-Inflicting (i.e., behaviours that reduce the likelihood ofpartner infidelity by inflicting costs on a partner).

Mate Retention in Ladies…

The goal of mate retention behaviour is to stop a partner from cheating on you or leaving the relationship. In humans, the ability of a woman to keep her partner has a significant impact on her success in reproduction. Additionally, it is advantageous for a woman to keep a cooperative spouse who is prepared to defend and provide for her, her children and her family. Women accomplish this by using mate retention strategies that are either cost inflicting or benefit provisioning.

Female perception of the intensity of controlling behaviours performed by both partners was the highest in couples where a woman assesses her own mate value (MV) as higher than her partner's MV and significantly different than in relationships where male MV exceeded those of the female (Danel et al.,2017).

The study by Lindova et al. (2019) revealed several interesting correlations between women behaviour in the presence of her partner and a potential rival, and the quality of their relationship:

1. Appearance-enhancing behaviours:

- Examples: Self-touch, hair flipping, grooming

- Correlation: Strongly positive with mutual adjustment and happiness of both partners

- Explanation: When women engaged in these behaviours, both partners reported higher levels of relationship satisfaction and adjustment. This suggests that a woman's efforts to enhance her appearance may positively impact the relationship dynamics.

2. Intimacy-inducing behaviour:

- Example: Long gaze

- Correlation:

a) Positive with the woman's own dyadic satisfaction

b) Positive with her partner's relationship adjustment

- Explanation: Women who engaged in prolonged eye contact reported higher satisfaction in their relationship. Additionally, the partner reported better satisfaction with the relationship. This implies that non-verbal intimacy cues can strengthen relationship bonds.

3. Direct guarding behaviour:

- Example: Brief looks at partner

- Correlation: Negative with partner's dyadic adjustment

- Explanation: When women frequently gave quick glances to their partners (possibly to monitor their behaviour), the partner reported lower levels of relationship satisfaction. This suggests that overt mate guarding behaviours might have a detrimental effect on relationship quality.

Overall implications:

The study highlights the significant role that female attractiveness and related behaviours play in mate retention, even in established romantic partnerships. It suggests that:

1. Behaviours that enhance a woman's attractiveness may serve as a positive mate retention strategy, benefiting both partners.

2. Subtle intimacy cues like prolonged eye contact can improve relationship satisfaction.

3. Overt mate guarding behaviours might have negative consequences for relationship quality.

These findings underscore the complex interplay between physical appearance, non-verbal behaviours and relationship dynamics in long-term partnerships. It is suggested that strategies focusing on self-enhancement and intimacy may be more effective for relationship maintenance than direct guarding behaviours.

Lindová (2022) researched on mate retention and found out some spicy details!

Women employ a variety of strategies to attract, entice and retain partners throughout different stages of relationships:

1. Appearance enhancement:

- Methods include cosmetic procedures, makeup use, stylish dressing, perfume application and attractive gestures.

- While effective for partner attraction and retention, these efforts are also subject to scrutiny and criticism from other women in competitive contexts.

2. Sexual practices:

- Women may engage in specific sexual behaviours, such as oral sex or feigning orgasms, as mate retention tactics.

Certainly. Let's delve deeper into the use of sexual practices as mate retention tactics:

1. Oral sex:

- Some women may use oral sex as a mate retention strategy.

- This can serve multiple purposes:

a) Increasing sexual satisfaction for the partner, potentially making the relationship more appealing.

b) Creating a sense of sexual novelty or adventure within the relationship.

c) Demonstrating sexual skill or enthusiasm, which may deter a partner from seeking sexual gratification elsewhere.

Research indicates a correlation between women's mate retention behaviours, emotional attachment, personality traits, and specific sexual practices. Women who frequently engage in loving and caring mate retention strategies tend to show more interest in and dedicate more time to performing oral sex on their partners. This tendency is particularly pronounced among women who report strong feelings of love for their partner. Additionally, women scoring higher in Agreeableness - a personality trait associated with consideration and kindness - are more likely to express greater interest in and spend more time performing oral sex **(Sela et al., 2015).**

2. Feigning orgasms:

- This practice involves pretending to reach a sexual climax during intimate encounters.

- Potential reasons for this behaviour in mate retention context include:

a) Boosting the partner's sexual confidence, making them feel more satisfied with the sexual relationship.

b) Avoiding potential relationship conflict or partner disappointment.

c) Reinforcing the partner's sense of sexual competence, which may reduce their likelihood of seeking other sexual partners.

Women may employ this behaviour of feigning sexual satisfaction, as a means of demonstrating their commitment and investment in the relationship. This strategy serves multiple purposes: it signals dedication to their partner, potentially discouraging infidelity and helps maintain harmony within the relationship. By appearing to have an orgasm, even when they haven't, women may aim to avoid conflicts and preserve peace in their partnership. Kaighobadi et al. (2012) suggested that such actions can be viewed as part of a broader set of mate retention tactics. These behaviours reflect the complex interplay between sexual dynamics, relationship maintenance and conflict avoidance in intimate partnerships. However, it's important to note that while these strategies may serve short-term goals, they might also raise questions about long-term relationship authenticity and sexual satisfaction.

3. Cost-inflicting strategies:

- Some women use tactics that impose costs on their partners or potential rivals.

- These may include:

a) Punishing the partner for perceived infidelity threats

b) Using indirect aggression, such as verbal disparagement of the partner or competitors

Research by Holden et al. (2014) reveals an interesting dynamic in marital relationships regarding mate retention behaviours. Husbands who perceive that their wives hold them in lower esteem are more likely to engage in cost-inflicting mate retention tactics. These behaviours are designed to make infidelity more difficult or costly for their wives. Conversely, husbands who feel highly valued by their wives are less likely to resort to such tactics. Furthermore, the study suggests that husbands who consider themselves to have high mate value tend to avoid these potentially harmful behaviours, as they might risk diminishing their wives' esteem for them. This pattern indicates that a husband's perception of his wife's regard for him, as well as his own sense of mate value, significantly influences his choice of mate retention strategies, with those feeling less valued or secure in the relationship more likely to employ potentially detrimental tactics.

This overview highlights the multifaceted nature of female mate retention strategies, ranging from self-enhancement to sexual behaviours and even potentially harmful tactics. It underscores the complexity of relationship dynamics and the various methods women might employ to maintain their partnerships. These strategies reflect evolutionary adaptations and social learning, but it's important to note that not all tactics are healthy or ethical in modern relationships. Some may lead to relationship strain or personal distress.

Attachment Patterns and Mate Retention

Individuals who are more anxiously attached tend to be more jealous (Kim, Feeney, Jakubika, 2017), overestimate the dangers to relationships and believe that their romantic partner is not as committed as they are (Mikulincer & Shaver, 2007). On the other hand, people who are more avoidantly attached report less chronic jealousy (Sharpsteen & Kirkpatrick, 1997) and are more aware of possible romantic partners outside of themselves (DeWall et al., 2011).

According to Barbaro et al. (2016) people who are more anxiously connected might engage in more frequent mate retention because they are more alert to signs of infidelity and possible breakup. On the other hand, people who are avoidant attached might perform less frequent mate retention because they are driven to avoid emotional connection and physical closeness with their romantic partner and ignore indicators that could be signs of cheating.

Mate retention in men…

Men employ a diverse array of mate retention strategies to maintain their romantic relationships and ensure their partner's fidelity. These tactics span a wide spectrum, from displays of affection to more assertive behaviours, all aimed at safeguarding the relationship against potential threats. Such strategies may include demonstrations of sexual prowess, providing emotional support or even attempts to limit their partner's social interactions with others. These behaviours reflect a complex interplay of psychological, socio cultural and biological factors that drive human mating dynamics. Understanding the motivations and mechanisms behind these mate retention efforts provides valuable insights into the evolutionary forces shaping human relationships. This multifaceted approach to relationship preservation underscores the intricate nature of human pair-bonding and the lengths to which individuals may go to protect their romantic partnerships.

Males often engage in behaviours aimed at preventing their romantic partners from engaging in infidelity or leaving the relationship. These actions are driven by evolutionary concerns: if a partner is unfaithful, a man risks being cuckolded and inadvertently investing resources in offspring that are not genetically his. Similarly, if the relationship ends, he loses both his previous investment in the partner and future reproductive opportunities with her.

However, some mate retention tactics can have negative consequences for the woman, as they may conflict with her interests (Shackelford et al., 2005). For instance, a man might try to control his partner's time or social interactions, effectively isolating her from potential support networks. He might also engage in public behaviours that diminish her self-esteem. Such strategies, while intended to preserve the relationship, can be detrimental to the woman's well-being, reducing her social support system and sense of self-worth.

Research by Miner et al. (2009) highlights that men also employ benefit-provisioning strategies to maintain their relationships and deter infidelity. These positive tactics can include lavishing partners with expensive gifts or offering sincere compliments about their appearance. Such behaviours aim to enhance the woman's satisfaction within the relationship, potentially reducing the likelihood of infidelity or relationship dissolution. The study also reveals interesting patterns in mate retention behaviours based on partner characteristics. Men paired with younger, more attractive women tend to engage in more mate retention behaviours compared to those with older, less attractive partners. Interestingly, a woman's mate value appears to influence the frequency of specific negative mate retention tactics used by her partner. Specifically, women with higher mate values report experiencing fewer partner-directed insults, a form of mate retention behaviour, than those with lower mate values.

Men employ various sexual and behavioural strategies in mate retention, with oral sex being one such tactic. Pham & Shackelford (2013) found that men who perceive a higher risk of partner infidelity report greater interest in and time spent performing oral sex on their partners. This behaviour appears to be specific to long-term relationships, as Backstrom et al. (2012) noted that men generally do not engage in oral sex during casual encounters like one-night stands, where the risk of long-term partner infidelity is minimal.

Hormonal factors also play a role in mate retention behaviours. Arnocky et al. (2018) demonstrated a positive correlation between testosterone levels and various mate retention efforts in men. Higher testosterone levels were associated with increased vigilance for potential rivals, possessive behaviours and attempts to enhance personal attractiveness to partners. This aligns with the known effects of testosterone on dominance, competitiveness and mating behaviour in males.

In comparison to men with higher Emotional Stability scores, men with lower scores report more cost-inflicting and more benefit-providing partner retention behaviours. Partners of men who lack emotional stability often complain about their partners' jealousy and irritability. As a result, males who exhibit higher levels of anxiety and temperament may be more likely to engage in mate retention behaviours due to their increased suspicion of infidelity.

The link between mate retention and relationship violence is evident in online contexts as well. Forcing the partner to share their social networking passwords, snooping into the partner's phone is a common site.Brem et al. (2015) examined mate retention tactics among users of the popular social networking site "Facebook". They found that individuals who monitored their partner's online activity and attempted to control their partner's online posts were more likely to aggress against their partners. In the most extreme cases, mating retention effort can tragically lead to intimate partner homicide (Kaighobadi et al. 2009).

The relationship between personality types and mate retention strategies is also interesting. Individuals who prioritiseprestige and dominance tend to employ mate retention tactics that align with their personality traits. Those inclined towards dominance are more likely to use cost-intensive, controlling strategies such as monitoring their partner's whereabouts, belittling potential rivals, and issuing threats to same-sex competitors. These tactics reflect the coercive and manipulative nature characteristic of dominant personalities. In contrast, individuals who value prestige are more prone to using benefit-provisioning strategies. These may include displays of affection or publicly acknowledging their relationship status. Such approaches are consistent with the cooperative, status-oriented nature of prestige-focused individuals, emphasising the building and maintenance of social alliances (Conlon, 2019).

The relationship between personality traits and mate retention strategies reveals intriguing patterns. Men whose partners exhibit higher levels of Conscientiousness tend to engage more frequently in benefit-provisioning mate retention behaviours. This could be attributed to the reliability and trustworthiness associated with conscientious partners, which may inspire more positive retention tactics from their male counterparts. For instance, these men might be more inclined to invest time and effort in the relationship, knowing their partner's dependable nature.Conversely, certain personality traits are linked to more negative mate retention behaviours. Men scoring lower on Agreeableness or Emotional Stability, or those with partners lower in Openness, are more likely to employ cost-inflicting mate retention tactics. These might include controlling or manipulative behaviours aimed at maintaining the relationship.

On the positive side, men who score higher in Agreeableness or Openness, or whose partners demonstrate higher Conscientiousness, tend to favor benefit-provisioning mate retention strategies. These could involve acts of kindness, emotional support or public displays of commitment (McKibbin et al., 2014).

Mate retention behaviours are influenced by various contextual factors. The success of mate poaching, for instance, depends heavily on the situation. Long-distance relationships and dating scenarios are particularly vulnerable to mate poaching attempts. Additionally, environments that encourage flirtatious behaviour, such as parties or conferences, may increase the likelihood of infidelity and successful mate poaching.

Choosing mate retention strategies is also linked to individual characteristics and relationship dynamics. Research indicates that both men and women with higher self-esteem and greater relationship satisfaction tend to employ more positive, benefit-provisioning behaviours to retain their partners. This suggests that individuals who feel secure in themselves and their relationships are likelier to use a benevolent approach to maintain their partnership.

Conversely, the use of negative, cost-inflicting behaviours in mate retention seems to be associated with perceived threats to the relationship. For example, men are more likely to engage in cost-inflicting behaviours when they suspect or know that their female partner has been unfaithful. This implies that the perception of infidelity risk may trigger more aggressive mate retention tactics.

In essence, the choice between benevolent and aggressive mate retention strategies appears to be influenced by a combination of individual factors, relationship quality, and perceived threats to the partnership.

CHAPTER – 12

Fear of the Alter... Gamophobia

"One should always be in love. That is the reason one should never marry."
-Oscar Wilde

Fear of marriage or commitment is a multifaceted emotional phenomenon that affects people's relationships and decisions in life. This dread, whether it stems from personal beliefs, cultural influences or past experiences, can have a major impact on an individual's capacity to fully engage in romantic relationships or make the leap into marriage. The fear of commitment can prevent intimacy and the development of strong, enduring bonds. It might be caused by worries about losing one's own independence or about future conflicts and obligations.

There are many extremely specific reasons why people fear marriage or commitment, many of which are impacted by cultural norms, personal experiences and beliefs. Some people could fear losing their freedom or autonomy because they see commitment as a possible danger to it. Some people may be afraid to commit to a new relationship because they are still carrying emotional scars from earlier relationships.

There's also the fear of falling short of what society considers a successful marriage or relationship or of not living up to expectations. This anxiety can be made worse by unrealistic expectations that are stoked by societal standards and media representations, which can lead to feelings of inadequacy or anxiety. Moreover, some people could experience underlying issues like commitment phobia.

Gamophobia is the dread of commitment in people. They frequently find it impossible to be in committed relationships because of this extreme anxiety. The Greek term for marriage is "gamos." "Phobos", a phobia, signifies fear.

Though the Diagnostic and Statistical Manual of Mental Disorders (DSM-5), published by the American Psychiatric Association and used by mental health practitioners to diagnose mental health issues, does not classify "gamophobia" as a distinct phobia yet. However, it's worth noting that specific phobias, including fears related to commitment or marriage, may fall under the broader category of specific phobiasif they meet certain criteria outlined in the DSM-5. These criteria include experiencing significant distress or impairment in daily functioning due to the fear and the fear being excessive or unreasonable.

More and more people are delaying getting married or not getting married at all. Despite research suggesting that men have historically found it more challengingto commit to marriage, more women are now choosing not to get married. Fears of losing one's identity, control or finances, as well as concerns about taking on adult responsibilities are some associated issues (Curtis & Susman 1994).

The relationships greatly influence our mental health and general well-being in our lives. A sense of security, emotional fulfilmentand belonging all are crucial for preserving mental health and can be found in strong, sustaining relationships. Strong and stablerelationships can be very helpful in providing emotional support during stressful or difficult situations, acting as a protective barrier against depressive, anxious or lonely sensations. On the other hand, strained or toxic relationships can be harmful to one's mental well-being. Emotional discomfort and poor self-worth can be exacerbated by toxic interactions that involve criticism, disagreement or lack of trust. People who are in abusive relationships- emotional, physical or verbal may suffer severe trauma and long-term psychological effects. In addition, relationship problems like breakups, divorces or conflicts with loved ones can aggravate pre-existing mental health conditions by evoking strong emotional reactions. These difficulties may result in depressive and anxious symptoms as well as emotions of loss, melancholy and loneliness.

Relationships are an essential aspect of human functioning that can impact a wide range of mental health consequences.Improving relationships improves mental health, but improving mental health does not reliably improve relationships (Braithwaite & Holt-Lunstad, 2017).

Research has illuminated the significant influence of personality traits on an individual's approach to romantic commitment and relationship status. A study by Apostolou and Tekeş (2023) revealed that certain personality characteristics are associated with a heightened fear of relationship commitment and a greater likelihood of being single. Specifically, individuals with lower levels of agreeableness, openness and self-reported mating performance, as well as those who perceive their relationship quality as poor, tend to exhibit a stronger fear of commitment in romantic relationships. Furthermore, the study uncovered a complex interplay between personality traits, mating performance and relationship outcomes. Lower levels of self-esteem, extraversion and openness were found to correlate with reduced mating performance. This diminished performance, in turn, was associated with an increased fear of relationship commitment and a higher probability of being single rather than in an intimate relationship.

According to attachment theory, a person's early relationships with their caretakers influence how they form attachment patterns. In adult relationships, those with an anxious or avoidant attachment style may find it difficult to commit. While avoidant attached people may fear intimacy and closeness, which causes them to completely avoid commitment, anxiously attached people may fear desertion and seek out continual reassurance. It turns out that those who identify with avoidant attachment style frequently worry about losing their independence or freedom and have negative views about relationships. They find commitment to be extremely repellent since it makes them feel trapped or dominated (Park et al., 2019).

People who have low self-esteem or a fear of rejection could put off starting a relationship because they worry that their partner would reject them or leave them. This fear may have its roots in feelings of worthlessness or rejection from the past. Individuals with a fear of rejection may struggle with vulnerability and intimacy in relationships. Fear of rejection can lead to self-sabotaging behaviours that undermine the relationship. Individuals may engage in behaviours such as pushing their partner away, creating unnecessary conflict or avoiding important conversations as a way to protect themselves from potential rejection.

It can also contribute to a pattern of seeking validation and reassurance from partners. Individuals may constantly seek approval and affirmation from their partner as a way to alleviate their anxiety about being rejected. Individuals who fear rejection may have difficulty expressing their needs and boundaries in the relationship. They may prioritise avoiding conflict or disagreement out of fear that it will lead to rejection or abandonment by their partner. This can result in unmet needs and unresolved issues within the relationship, further exacerbating feelings of dissatisfaction and insecurity (Downey et al., 1999).

Some are afraid to commit to a relationship because they don't think they can live up to their partner's expectations or see the relationship through to the end. Perfectionism or a lack of self-confidence may cause this dread of failing in the relationship.

Perfectionism was found to have a negative effect on relationship satisfaction. Since perfectionism frequently breeds irrational expectations and a fear of falling short of them, it can be a major obstacle to completely committing to romantic relationships. Perfectionists often have unrealistic expectations for both themselves and their partners, which causes ongoing tension and discontent in the relationship.

This anxiety of falling short of an idealisedstandard can take many different forms. Perfectionism can cause people to completely avoid committing to a relationship because they worry that neither they nor their partner will ever match up perfectionism. They might also put off getting into relationship until they find the "perfect" partner or until they think the partner is flawless, which can lead to lost chances for deep and lasting relationships (Stoeber, 2012).

Individuals with personality traits like independence, autonomy and self-sufficiency might put their own space and freedom over committing to a long-term relationship. These people could feel restricted by the demands of a committed relationship or fear losing their independence. Growing up in a family whereindependence was restricted and an individual felt out of control because of controlling parents or growing up in a home whereemotional needs weren't satisfied and it was taught to rely on oneself from an early age,contribute to the development of the fear of losing your independence. The fear of losing independence will often become more apparent once an individual starts to grow closer to someone and have difficulty trusting that the other person will meet their needs since it didn't feel safe to do so in the past.

Fear of commitment in romantic relationships can be impacted by various psychological factors, including certain psychological disorders. A person's capacity to commit in romantic relationships can be greatly impacted by psychological disorders such as Generalised Anxiety Disorder (GAD), Avoidant Personality Disorder (AvPD) and Borderline Personality Disorder (BPD).

Patients with borderline personality disorder (BPD) suffer greatly from their unstable interpersonal relationships. In the case of BPD, individuals may worry about being rejected or abandoned by their relationships, which can result in a pervasive fear of commitment due to significant anxieties of abandonment and unstable self-image.

Individuals with Borderline Personality Disorder (BPD) often struggle to maintain a stable perception of their partner's trustworthiness, particularly during threatening situations. This difficulty extends beyond relationship-specific threats and can significantly impact their interpersonal relationships. Interestingly, displays of tenderness in the relationship may serve as a protective factor, potentially mitigating some of these challenges (Miano, 2017)..Similarly, anxiety can pose significant obstacles to forming and maintaining healthy romantic relationships. People with anxiety disorders may experience intense worry and fear about the future of their relationships, leading to commitment issues. This anxiety can manifest in various ways, including avoidance of relationships altogether, sabotaging existing partnerships or feeling trapped and suffocated within a committed relationship. This phenomenon is often referred to as attachment anxiety (Joel et al., 2011).

Two distinct dimensions of relationship commitment are approach commitment and avoidance commitment. These concepts are rooted in the psychological framework of approach and avoidance motivations, which are fundamental drivers of human behaviour. Approach commitment refers to the positive motivation to maintain and nurture a relationship. It's characterized by the focus on the potential benefits and rewards that the relationship can offer in the future. Individuals with high approach commitment are drawn to their partner and the relationship because of the positive experiences, emotional fulfilment and personal growth they anticipate. This type of commitment is proactive and optimistic, driven by the desire to create and enjoy positive outcomes within the relationship.

On the other hand, avoidance commitment is motivated by the desire to prevent negative consequences associated with ending the relationship. This form of commitment is more reactive and focused on avoiding potential losses or drawbacks that might result from a breakup. People with high avoidance commitment may stay in a relationship not necessarily because of its positive aspects, but rather due to fears about the emotional, social or practical costs of dissolution.

To illustrate:

- An individual with high approach commitment might say, "I'm excited about building a future with my partner and growing together."

- Someone with high avoidance commitment might think, "I don't want to end this relationship because being single would be too difficult or lonely."

It's important to note that these two types of commitment are not mutually exclusive. Individuals can experience both approach and avoidance commitment simultaneously, though one may be stronger than the other. The balance between these two forms of commitment can significantly influence relationship satisfaction, longevity and overall quality (Strachman & Gable, 2006).

In conclusion, a number of psychological factors, including attachment anxiety, prior experiences of rejection or abandonment, and underlying mental health issues like avoidant or borderline personality disorder, might contribute to the fear of commitment in romantic relationships. This anxiety may show itself as a refusal to give a commitment to a relationship, or even a complete avoidance of romantic relationships. It frequently takes reflection, counseling and a willingness to face and treat underlying fears and past traumas to overcome a fear of commitment.

Fear of Being Single.... the opposite of fear of commitment in romantic relationship

You might have heard people saying "I will die single" or "I will be alone and lonely when I am old". All these remarks are nothing but portray a fear of being single. Fear of being single (FOBS) is characterized by worry, anxiety, or anguish about what it would be like to be single in the future or right now. It is commonly linked to "settling for less" in romantic relationships. Stronger FOBS predicts that men and women will be more interested in dating less responsive and physically beautiful possibilities and that they will be less likely to initiate breakups with unsatisfactory partners once they are in a relationship. According to Spielmann et al. (2013), those with higher FOBS also have a tendency to indicate interest in a greater number of people, which leads to a less selective matching technique during speed dating.

The fear of being single is a complicated psychological condition that has a significant impact on people's attitudes and actions in romantic relationships. A basic part of human nature is the need for connection and companionship, but for other people, the mere idea of being by themselves causes them great fear and worry. This anxiety can take many different forms, affecting people's sense of fulfilment and self-worth as well as how they negotiate intimate relationships.

Research has illuminated the significant impact that fear of being single can have on individuals' romantic choices and behaviours. This apprehension about solitude can profoundly shape one's approach to relationships, often leading to compromised standards in partner selection. Studies have consistently demonstrated that individuals with a higher fear of being single tend to express romantic interest in potential partners who are less responsive or less physically attractive, suggesting a willingness to settle for less-than-ideal matches.

This fear can manifest as a powerful motivator, compelling individuals to prioritise relationship status over relationship quality. As a result, those grappling with this fear may find themselves overlooking incompatibilities, dismissing warning signs or enduring unsatisfactory relationship dynamics. The underlying drive to avoid the perceived desolation of singlehood can lead to a pattern of accepting subpar relationships or remaining in stagnant partnerships.

Interestingly, while the fear of being single predicted less selectivity in expressing romantic interest, it did not influence the romantic interest received from others. This suggests that the impact of this fear is primarily internal, affecting one's own choices rather than one's desirability to potential partners.

Longing for ex-partners out of fear of being single is a common phenomenon that highlights the significant impact of the fear of solitude on romantic relationships. When faced with the prospect of being alone, individuals may romanticisepast relationships and idealisetheir ex-partners, viewing them through a nostalgic rose tinted lens. This longing often arises from a deep-seated fear of loneliness and a desire for emotional security and companionship. Memories of past connections, combined with the uncertainty of the future, can create a powerful pull towards familiar comforts, even if those relationships were ultimately unhealthy or incompatible.

Research conducted by Spielmann and colleagues (2013, 2016) provides compelling insights into the intricate relationship between the fear of being single and post-breakup dynamics. Their findings reveal that individuals with a heightened fear of solitude tend to experience more intense cravings for their former partners. Notably, this fear of being single was observed to increase following a breakup, regardless of which partner initiated the separation. The study's within-day analysis yielded particularly illuminating results. On days when individuals reported a more pronounced fear of being alone, they also experienced a stronger desire for their ex-partner and were more likely to engage in attempts to rekindle the relationship. Interestingly, the researchers found that while the fear of being single intensified longing and renewalattempts over time, the reverse was not true; longing for an ex-partner and attempts to reconnect did not significantly impact the fear of being single.

These findings underscore the fear of being single as a crucial concept in understanding the romantic detachment process. It appears to be a driving force behind post-breakup behaviours and emotions, rather than a consequence of them. This research offers valuable insights into the psychological mechanisms at play during relationship dissolution and recovery, highlighting the profound influence that the fear of solitude can exert on an individual's emotional responses and actions following a breakup.

The Bridget Jones effect: The relationship between exposure to romantic media content and fear of being single among emerging adults.

Research by Timmermans et al. (2019) illuminates the significant influence of romantic media consumption on individuals' attitudes towards singlehood, particularly highlighting its impact on the fear of being single (FOBS). This study reveals a notable correlation between higher consumption of romantic media—including films, television shows and literature in the romantic comedy and drama genres and an increased fear of being single. This association is particularly pronounced among single women.

The research suggests that exposure to romantic media can be pivotal in shaping individuals' perceptions of relationships and singlehood. The media often present idealized portrayals of romantic love, framing it as thequintessential source of personal fulfilment and happiness. Such depictions can foster unrealistic expectations about relationships and inadvertently promote the notion that one's worth and life satisfaction are intrinsically tied to romantic partnership.

Consequently, individuals who consume a high volume of romantic media may internalise these messages, leading to an elevated fear of being single. This internalization can manifest as feelings of inadequacy or anxiety about being alone, particularly among those who are not currently in a romantic relationship.

Recent research has shed light on the complex interplay between attachment anxiety, fear of being single and relationship behaviours. Sakman et al. (2021) found a significant association between higher levels of attachment anxiety and an increased fear of being single. This heightened fear, in turn, was linked to a greater likelihood of engaging in infidelity. These findings suggest that individuals with high attachment anxiety may be more prone to pursuing extradyadic relationships as a strategic response to their intense fear of solitude. This behaviour could be interpreted as a form of "bet-hedging," where individuals attempt to mitigate the perceived risk of future singlehood by maintaining alternative romantic options.

Complementing these findings, Spielmann et al. (2016) observed day-to-day fluctuations in the fear of being single and its impact on post-breakup behaviours. Their study revealed that on days when individuals experienced a more intense fear of being single, they also reported stronger longing for ex-partners and increased attempts to rekindle past relationships. Importantly, the researchers found that this relationship was unidirectional: while the fear of being single amplified longing and reconciliation attempts over time, these behaviours did not reciprocally influence the fear of being single.

Together, these studies illuminate the profound influence that the fear of being single can exert on relationship dynamics. Whether manifesting as a driver of infidelity in ongoing relationships or as a catalyst for attempting to revive past connections, this fear appears to be a potent force shaping romantic behaviours and decisions. These insights underscore the importance of addressing attachment-related anxieties and fears surrounding singlehood in fostering healthier relationship patterns and personal well-being.

CHAPTER – 13

Single Shaming

Find someone naa? Don't tell us you do not have a boyfriend. You are too good-looking to be single. You must be dating someone, you just don't want to disclose. Download some dating apps; your biological clock is ticking. You will be an old grumpy lady with cats. All these sentences are not uncommon for a single woman or man and sometimes one gets to hear these sentences in the form of a snarky comment and sometimes in the form of concern. But believe me, I am a single woman in her thirties and I can honestly tell you that no one chooses to stay single if one finds what one desires for. So, a single person thinks about their status much more than concerned people do. Let's delve a little deeper into the much prevalent concept of single shaming.

The demand to fit in with society's conventions, especially when it comes to relationships, has increased in today's connected world of social media and digital platforms. Even while conversations about inclusion and inclusivity have been stronger recently, single shaming is still a problem that is both common and frequently ignored. The practice of stigmatising people for being single, or "single shaming," takes the form of imperceptible comments, social norms and cultural narratives that conflate romantic connection with the only source of fulfilment. This phenomenon undercuts the variety of avenues to personal fulfilment and satisfaction in addition to marginalising those who opt to stay unmarried or unpartnered.

Single shaming is when someone is negatively judged for not being in a relationship or for not marrying at a certain age as per social norms. Shamers act differently when they are around single people. People often assume that single people are boring and lonely. People sometimes feel sorry for single people because they are single and they often hear "shaming phrases" from others such as "You must be so lonely!" and "You'll meet someone soon!"

Single individuals often face unfounded stereotypes and misconceptions about their lives and character. These may include the notion that their existence is somehow 'tragic', that married people possess a unique life perspective unavailable to singles or that choosing to remain unmarried is inherently selfish. Such stereotypes are not only inaccurate but can also be harmful.

The societal pressure and stigma associated with being single can lead to internalised shame, significantly impacting an individual's self-esteem and self-perception. This is particularly challenging for those who aspire to find a life partner but have not yet done so.

Moreover, the cultural emphasis on certain life milestones, such as marriage and parenthood, can create additional stress for single individuals. When these expectations are not met, it may lead to feelings of inadequacy or failure, despite the fact that such milestones are not universal measures of personal success or fulfilment.

Research in the field of social psychology has shed light on the pervasive nature of "singlism," a term coined to describe the stigmatisation and prejudice faced by single individuals, particularly in the marriage-centric culture of the United States (DePaulo, 2014). Recent studies have revealed a disturbing trend: discrimination against singles is often considered more socially acceptable than prejudice towards other marginalisedgroups, including foreign nationals and sexual minorities (Fisher & Sakaluk, 2020).

The stark contrast in societal perceptions of married versus single individuals is evident in research conducted by DePaulo and Morris (2006). Their findings indicate that people tend to associate married individuals with positive attributes such as maturity, stability, honesty, happiness, kindness and loving nature. Conversely, single individuals are more likely to be characterised by negative traits, including immaturity, insecurity, self-centeredness, sadness, loneliness and unattractiveness.

Notably, these unfavorable stereotypes become even more pronounced when applied to older single individuals, with the negativity intensifying for those around 40 years of age compared to those in their mid-twenties. However, it is crucial to emphasize that these perceptions are largely baseless stereotypes that do not accurately reflect the diverse realities of single individuals' lives.

The interplay between relationship status and mental health is intricate and multifaceted. While a nurturing and supportive romantic partnership can indeed provide emotional stability and a sense of belonging, it's crucial to recognisethat one's relationship status is not the sole determinant of mental well-being.

Individuals in relationships may encounter their own set of challenges, just as single individuals can lead fulfilling and mentally healthy lives. For some, single life offers unique opportunities for personal growth, self-exploration and thecultivation of independence—all of which can significantly contribute to positive mental health outcomes.

The state of being single can serve as a fertile ground for self-discovery and personal development. It allows individuals the freedom to focus on their own needs, interests and aspirations without the necessity of compromising for a partner. This autonomy can foster resilience, self-reliance and a strong sense of identity, which are all integral components of robust mental health.

Ultimately, mental well-being is influenced by a complex interplay of factors, of which relationship status is but one element. The key lies in fostering meaningful connections, pursuing personal growth and maintaining a balanced lifestyle, regardless of whether one is in a romantic partnership or enjoying a single life.

However, when people believe they are not living up to society's norms, pressure from society and prejudices about being single can cause feelings of inadequacy, loneliness and even guilt. On the other hand, although relationships can provide intimacy, affection and support, they can also bring about tensions and disputes that have an adverse effect on mental health. An individual's emotional health may suffer from unhealthy relationships that involve violence, codependency or poor communication.

A comprehensive analysis of both longitudinal and cross-sectional data has revealed a nuanced interplay between relationship status, relationship quality and mental health outcomes for both genders. The findings suggest that the mere presence of a romantic partnership is not inherently beneficial to mental well-being. Rather, it is the quality of the relationship that serves as a critical determinant of mental health outcomes.

Notably, only high-quality relationships were associated with superior mental health compared to single status. This underscores the importance of the nature and dynamics of a partnership rather than its mere existence. The study further illuminated a gender-specific effect, particularly concerning anxiety levels in women. Interestingly, women in low-quality relationships reported higher levels of anxiety compared to their single counterparts, highlighting the potential detrimental effects of unsatisfactory partnerships on mental health (Leach et al., 2013).

Fear of being alone may be a powerful incentive for settling into romantic relationships, frequently pushing people to accept less than they trul0y want or deserve. Social pressures, uncertainties inside oneself and the perceived shame attached to being single all contribute to this dread. According to research, people who are afraid of being single might lower their standards, ignore warning signs or continue in unhealthy relationships in order to avoid feeling uncomfortable by themselves. This practice, called "settling," can have serious repercussions for people as well as their relationships. In the long term, settling frequently results in unhappiness, bitterness and lack of fulfilment. Additionally, because people may find it difficult to set boundaries and express their needs as they are afraid of being alone, it can reinforce unhealthy patterns of relationship dynamics (Spielmann et al., 2013).

The results of the research show that social pressures and the fear of being single (FOBS) interact in a complex way, with gender variances and clear distinctions between peer and parental impacts. According to the study, people feel more pressure to form relationships from their parents and relatives than from their peers. This familial pressure, which is more noticeable in women, emphasizes the long-lasting impact of cultural norms and conventional expectations about romantic relationships in familial settings. In addition, women scored higher on the fear of being single (FOBS) measure than males did, and they also reported feeling more pressure from parents and relatives. This implies that women's perceptions and actions in romantic context may be influenced by society's expectations about their relationship status, which could lead to increased anxiety about being single (Sprecher& Felmlee, 2021).

A comprehensive analysis of mental health outcomes across relationship statuses has revealed significant disparities between single individuals and their partnered counterparts. The research indicates that those who are single tend to exhibit higher rates of various psychological challenges. Specifically, single individuals were found to report elevated levels of depression, anxiety and mood disorders compared to those in relationships. Additionally, they demonstrated a greater propensity for adjustment problems and other manifestations of psychological distress.

The study also highlighted a notable correlation between single status and substance use issues, particularly concerning alcohol consumption. Single individuals were observed to have a higher incidence of alcohol-related problems, suggesting a potential link between relationship status and patterns of substance use (Braithwaite et al., 2010).

Continuous exposure to messages that indicate being single is odd or undesirable can have a profound effect on how people view themselves.

The pervasive societal emphasis on romantic relationships can have profound psychological effects on single individuals. When people internalize messages that implicitly or explicitly prioritize partnered status, it can initiate a detrimental cycle of self-doubt and diminished self-worth. Single individuals may begin to equate their personal valueswith their relationship status, leading to feelings of inadequacy and unworthiness. This erosion of self-esteem can permeate various aspects of their lives, influencing social interactions, decision-making processes and overall well-being. Consequently, those who experience stigma related to their single status may struggle to recognisetheir intrinsic worth and to cultivate a sense of fulfilment independent of romantic partnerships.

The phenomenon of "single shaming" exacerbates the already prevalent feelings of alienation and loneliness often experienced by single individuals, potentially intensifying symptoms of anxiety and depression. The social stigma associated with being unpartnered can amplify these negative emotions, fostering a sense of isolation and misunderstanding. As single individuals encounter criticism and judgment regarding their relationship status, they may internalize the notion that they are somehow deficient or that they don't belong in society's relationship-centric narrative. This perceived social exclusion can significantly impact mental health, potentially leading to elevated levels of anxiety and depressive symptoms.

Moreover, the fear of rejection or judgment stemming from their single status may deter individuals from seeking support or forming meaningful connections, thereby exacerbating their feelings of loneliness. This creates a vicious cycle where single shaming contributes to increased isolation and emotional distress, ultimately compromising mental health and quality of life. Breaking this cycle requires challenging societal norms, promoting self-acceptance and fostering a more inclusive understanding of diverse relationship statuses and life paths.

People who are single face a great deal of pressure to follow society's expectations about relationships, even if they are not personally ready or interested. This pressure results from the worry that one would be judged or criticised for not adhering to the accepted standard of being in a love relationship. As a result, people could feel pressured to pursue relationships even when they are not emotionally ready or truly interested in doing so in order to avoid social scrutiny.

Stress and anxiety can be brought on by this internal struggle between their own desires and those of others. Additionally, the pressure to fit in might result in relationships that are unhealthy or unfulfilling for either party, which can instigate mental pain. In the end, single shaming perpetuates a society in which people value social approval more than their own genuine wants and wishes, contributing to a cycle of emotional turmoil and dissatisfaction.

The persistent exposure to societal messages that tie one's relationship status to personal worth can profoundly impact an individual's sense of identity and self-value. When bombarded with such notions regularly, people may internalisethese ideas, leading to a detrimental cycle of self-doubt and insecurity.

This internalisation process can cause individuals to view their single status as a reflection of personal inadequacies or flaws, fostering feelings of guilt and unworthiness. The resulting erosion of confidence and self-esteem can be pervasive, making it challenging for them torecognisee and assert their intrinsic value independent of romantic partnerships.

Consequently, individuals may struggle to cultivate a positive self-image, regardless of their relationship status. This difficulty in affirming their worth can lead to a pervasive sense of insecurity and diminished self-esteem, which may permeate various aspects of their lives.

The far-reaching implications of this phenomenon can significantly hinder personal growth and the development of a robust, positive self-identity. Ultimately, the internalization of societal stigma surrounding singlehood can create a self-perpetuating cycle of negative self-perception, impacting an individual's overall well-being and life satisfaction.

The pervasive nature of single shaming extends beyond internal perceptions, significantly impacting individuals' social behaviours and external interactions. The constant scrutiny and stigma associated with being unpartnered can engender social anxiety and heightened self-consciousness.

In social settings, individuals may experience increased apprehension and discomfort, fearing judgment or ridicule based on their relationship status. This anxiety can lead to a pattern of social withdrawal, as people attempt to avoid perceived criticism or embarrassment. Paradoxically, this self-imposed isolation often exacerbates feelings of loneliness and disconnection, as individuals deprive themselves of opportunities for support and meaningful connections.

This cycle of social disengagement can become self-perpetuating, progressively eroding one's mental health and social functioning over time. The cumulative effect of single shaming may thus create a downward spiral of increasing isolation and emotional distress. In response to the emotional turmoil and social pressure associated with being single, individuals may resort to maladaptive coping mechanisms. Common examples include substance abuse, excessive spending or unhealthy eating habits. These behaviours serve as temporary distractions from feelings of inadequacy, loneliness and social isolation, providing momentary relief from the distress induced by single shaming.

Substance addiction as a kind of self-medication to dull emotional pain and reduce stress can entail alcohol, narcotics or other addictive substances. In the same way, overindulging in food might serve as a momentary diversion from unfavorable feelings and thoughts. Similarly, obsessive shopping or excessivespending onmaterial goods can provide a fleeting sense of control or satisfaction in the face of perceived social judgment.

Single shaming causes stress and emotional strain that can lead to physical ailments and mental health problems that are damaging to general well-being. People who are constantly under social pressure and shame because of their relationship status can suffer from a variety of health conditions, such as immune system weakness, migraines and sleeplessness. Single-shaming-related persistent stress and worry can lead to tension headaches, which exacerbate discomfort and make it challenging to go about everyday tasks. Furthermore, the emotional upheaval brought on by feeling rejected or condemned might interfere with sleep cycles, resulting in insomnia or other sleep problems. This sleep deprivation exacerbates the person's general sense of well-being by adding to feelings of exhaustion, irritability and cognitive impairment.

Furthermore, a reduced immune system, which leaves people more vulnerable to infections and illnesses, has been linked to long-term stress. Prolonged stress has a physiological cost that can impair the body's defences against pathogens, resulting in recurrent infections and extended recuperation times. In addition to adding to personal misery, these outward signs of solitary shaming intensify the vicious cycle of tension and depressive feelings. Physical symptoms can worsen feelings of inadequacy and loneliness and make it more difficult for people to handle social pressure. Therefore, addressing solitary shaming bodily manifestations is crucial to fostering holistic well-being and reducing the harmful consequences that societal stigma has on people's health.

In conclusion, the practice of single shaming exerts a profound and detrimental impact on individuals' mental, emotional and physical well-being. Chronic exposure to stigmatising messages and social pressures engenders a cascade of adverse effects, including diminished self-esteem, heightened anxiety and depression, and the adoption of maladaptive coping mechanisms. Moreover, single shaming intensifies feelings of isolation, loneliness and self-consciousness, thereby impeding meaningful social interactions and the maintenance of a positive self-concept. The physiological consequences of sustained stress and emotional distress further compound the negative ramifications of single shaming on overall health.

Addressing this pervasive issue necessitates a multifaceted approach. It is imperative to challenge societal norms, promote acceptance of diverse lifestyles and provide resources and support systems to help individuals navigate the psychological and emotional challenges associated with single shaming. By cultivating a culture of inclusivity and empathy, we can mitigate the harmful effects of this phenomenon and foster a more supportive and equitable society for all individuals, regardless of their relationship status.

"Singles studies? What's that? It is an area of study that should exist but does not."
—Bella DePaulo

Historically, the field of relationship science has predominantly focused on coupled (married or partnered) relationships and parent-child dynamics (Berscheid, 1999). However, this narrow scope has inadvertently marginalized a significant and growing demographic within adult populations: single individuals. Often misconceived as isolated entities, unmarried adults represent an understudied yet increasingly prominent segment of society that warrants deeper investigation and understanding (DePaulo, 2014; Fry and Parker, 2021).

CHAPTER – 14

Long Distance Relationships

"Distance makes the heart grow fonder"

or

"Out of sight, out of mind"

When two people are not in the same area and cannot physically visit one another without significant travel costs, advance planning or disruption to their routine, they are said to be in a long-distance relationship. Any pair who resides in the same city, town or region, does not need to make travel arrangements, incur unusual costs and is able to see each other in person on a regular basis is considered to be in a geographically closerelationship. Notably, every couple's version of these relationships may be unique. It doesn't matter if a pair calls each other their "boyfriend" and "girlfriend," the significant other or just have an undefined but understood committed connection; it is still a case of long distance relationship(Peterson, 2014).

In the world of romantic relationships, long-distance relationships offer special opportunities as well as obstacles. In today's more interconnected world, where people frequently have to manage professional or educational obligations across many cities or even nations, long-distance relationships are becoming more prevalent. These relationships are fueled by emotional closeness, communicationand a common desire to keep the connection going even despite the physical distance.

Even the greatest relationships can become strained by the lack of frequent personal interactions as well as the difficulties of juggling different schedules and time zones. However, many couples discover that despite their differences, the challenges of being apart may strengthen their bond and increase their admiration for one another in surprising ways.

Stanley and Markman's (2013) findings align with the hypothesisedoutcomes regarding long-distance relationships. Their research reveals that couples in such arrangements experience heightened levels of "Perceived Togetherness." This phenomenon is likely attributed to the quality of interactions during the limited occasions when these couples have the opportunity to reunite and spend time together. The intensity and significance of these encounters appear to foster a stronger sense of connection despite the physical distance that typically separates them.

Research by Kelmer et al. (2013) reveals intriguing insights into long-distance relationships. Contrary to common assumptions, individuals in these relationships reported higher levels of dedication and overall relationship quality compared to those in close-proximity partnerships. They also experienced a diminished sense of feeling trapped or constrained. Interestingly, both groups exhibited similar perceptions of material constraints. Moreover, the study found that those in long-distance relationships were equally likely as their close-proximity counterparts to anticipate a potential end to their relationship at its onset. These findings challenge conventional wisdom about the viability and satisfaction levels of long-distance romantic connections.

In long-distance relationships, technology plays a crucial role in bridging the physical divide and preserving emotional intimacy. Partners can maintain real-time connection regardless of geographic distance thanks to the development of numerous communication platforms and digital tools. With the use of video chatting apps like Skype, FaceTime and Zoom, couples can communicate face-to-face and see each other's emotions and body language, which helps to build intimacy and a sense of closeness.

Apps for instant messaging, like Telegram and WhatsApp, allow couples to communicate constantly and easily exchange thoughts, feelings and daily experiences. Social media sites give couples a way to stay connected in each other's lives even when they are separated by distance by giving them a place to share updates, pictures and videos. Additionally, technology provides innovative methods to improve the love experience, including virtual date nights, online gaming together or watching movies simultaneously through streaming services.

Video chat technology provides a unique opportunity for couples to maintain a sense of shared presence despite physical separation, fostering closeness regardless of their relationship status. While this medium offers significant benefits, Neustaedter and Greenberg (2012) identified several challenges that couples must navigate when using video chat. These challenges fall into three main categories: contextual (such as differences in partners' locations and time zones), technical (including issues related to mobility, audio/video quality and network connectivity) and personal (notably, the limitation that most individuals require physical proximity for intimate sexual interactions).

Research by Merolla (2012) indicates that couples who engage in face-to-face interactions tend to experience higher levels of relationship satisfaction. Conversely, Kelmer et al. (2013) found that individuals in long-distance relationships report superior overall relationship quality. These seemingly contradictory findings suggest a more nuanced interpretation: the quality of a relationship and the satisfaction derived from it may be more contingent on the individuals involved rather than the nature of the relationship itself. This perspective implies that factors such as personal compatibility, communication skills and emotional intelligence might play a more significant role in determining relationship outcomes than the physical proximity of the partners.

Lee and Pistols (2012) research reveals intriguing differences in the dynamics of geographically close relationships (GCRs) and long-distance relationships (LDRs). In GCRs, self-disclosure positively correlated with idealization, while the opposite was true for LDRs. Both relationship types exhibited negative associations between insecure attachment and idealisation, as well as between insecure attachment and satisfaction. The study found that individuals with higher insecure attachment (both anxious and avoidant) tend to disclose less, idealisetheir partner less and experience lower relationship satisfaction, regardless of relationship type.

Interestingly, idealisationwas positively linked to satisfaction in both GCRs and LDRs. A unique finding for LDRs showed that individuals with higher insecure attachment were more prone to gossip. Furthermore, the impact of self-disclosure on idealisationdiffered between relationship types: in GCRs, higher self-disclosure and insecure attachment led to increased idealisation, while in LDRs, it resulted in decreased idealisation.

The prevalence of technology in modern relationships has unexpectedly led to complex emotional dynamics in long-distance romantic relationships. Despitethe increased connectivity offered by digital platforms, long distance relationships appear to be experiencing heightened levels of partner idealization, relational uncertainty and jealousy. This paradoxical situation may arise from the limitations of virtual communication, which can create gaps in understanding and foster unrealistic expectations. The absence of regular physical interaction might lead partners to fill in these gaps with idealized perceptions, potentially setting the stage for future disappointment. Additionally, the reduced daily involvement in each other's lives can breed uncertainty about the relationship's status and future. The constant awareness of the physical distance, coupled with the ability to glimpse into each other's separate lives through social media, may fuel jealousy and insecurity. Technology bridges the physical gap, it may inadvertently amplify emotional challenges in long-distance relationships.

The physical separation inherent in long-distance relationships often engenders profound feelings of loneliness and isolation for both partners. Firmin et al. (2014) highlight that this sense of solitude is particularly acute during significant life events when support and companionship are most crucial. The absence of a partner's physical presence can leave individuals grappling with a persistent void, whether celebrating achievements, facing challenges or simply yearning for the comfort of their loved one's company. This emotional chasm can intensify feelings of desolation and longing, potentially fostering a sense of estrangement from one's partner. Despite concerted efforts to maintain open lines of communication and connection, the physical distance creates an emotional gulf that proves challenging to bridge.

Relationships that are long-distance can be stressful and ambiguous, and that can negatively affect people's mental health. Anxiety and sadness can flourish in an environment where physical separation must be constantly navigated and communication and connection is difficult to maintain. These unfavourable feelings might be made worse by worries about trust and faithfulness, as well as uncertainty about the relationship's future, which can increase tension and discontent. Furthermore, when people struggle with the constant difficulties and sacrifices needed to keep the relationship running, the extended nature of distance can exacerbate these emotions over time. Because of this, people in long-distance relationships may have a variety of mental health problems, such as increased anxiety and mood disorders to a general decrease in life satisfaction.

Long-distance relationships initially appear less satisfying than geographically close relationships due to limited face-to-face interaction, potential communication challenges and increased financial burdens, as noted by Stafford and Merolla (2007). These stressors can potentially lead to psychological effects stemming from physical separation, including concerns about loyalty, fidelity and commitment.

Paradoxically, research by Kelmer et al. (2013) reveals that individuals in long-distance romantic relationships report higher levels of relationship adjustment and dedication. The geographical distance often necessitates a greater degree of commitment and adaptability from both partners. However, Ellis and Ledbetter (2015) point out that these required adjustments can sometimes result in relational turbulence. This complex interplay of factors suggests that while long distance relationships face unique challenges, they also foster heightened commitment and relationship quality, although with the potential for increased relational instability due to the ongoing adaptations required to maintain the connection across distance.

Research indicates that attitudes toward long-distance romantic relationships are significantly influenced by personal observations, others' opinions, past experiences and media portrayals. Maucione (2023) notes that while apredisposition towardslong distance exists, many young adults engage in these relationships despite potential reservations.

To navigate the unique challenges of long distance, partners employ various coping strategies. Firmin et al. (2014) identified techniques such as accurately interpreting text-based communication tone, enhancing communication efforts and committing to additional relationship work. The effectiveness of coping strategies varies based on the relationship's stress level. Maguire and Kinney (2010) found that in low-distress long-distance relationships, the perceived helpfulness of joint problem-solving was a key predictor of satisfaction. Conversely, in high-distress situations, the perceived helpfulness of openness emerged as a critical factor for relationship satisfaction.

Results also indicated that participants in short-term long-distance relationships reported higher levels of personal commitment than participants in long-term long-distance relationships (Gonzalez, 2011). Personal and perceived partner commitment and trust as predictors of relationship satisfaction in long-distance and proximally short dating relationships.

In long-distance romantic relationships, jealousy is a common and frequently difficult emotion that arises from the fear of losing one's partner to someone else or from feeling inadequate in comparison to others in their lover's life. Feelings of uncertainty can be made worse by the physical distance between couples because there may be fewer possibilities for assurance and intention clarity. Emotions of envy and mistrust can be exacerbated by elements like social circle differences, lack of visibility into each other's everyday lives and linguistic or cultural obstacles. Furthermore, the lack of physical presence might facilitate the emergence of illogical beliefs and suspicions, which can cause arguments and pressure in the partnership.

While anxious attachment has been identified as a key contributor to romantic jealousy among young adults in long-distance relationships, avoidant attachment appears to have little impact on such feelings (Tomasoa & Wulandari, 2024). The transition from a long-distance relationship to proximity brings about various challenges. These include a perceived loss of autonomy, an influx of both positive and negative information about the partner, difficulties in time management and an increase in conflict and jealousy. Interestingly, the desirable aspects of long-distance relationships, such as personal autonomy and the excitement of novelty, often diminish upon reunion and are subsequently missed. Stafford et al. (2006) found that individuals whose relationships ended after reuniting were more likely to report missing these distinct features of long-distance relationships.

Retroactive Jealousy in Long Distance Relationships-

In long-distance relationships, retroactive jealousy—a condition marked by compulsive thoughts and anxiety about a partner's previous relationships or experiences can be especially difficult to deal with. Feelings of unease and doubt are heightened by physical separation, which also facilitates the infiltration of intrusive thoughts on a partner's history. People in long distance relationships could find themselves obsessing over hypothetical situations or reading the past negatively by sometimes online stalking of social media accounts if there aren't regular interactions to offer comfort and perspective.

In long distance relationships, partners are made to stay engaged, a process known as relationship maintenance behaviours (RMBs).

The actions couples take to maintain and stop their intimate relationships from deteriorating are known as relationship maintenance behaviour (Ogolsky & Stafford, 2023).

Maintenance behaviours improve interaction and foster strong relationships between partners. Maintenance behaviours can be positive and negative in nature. Positive romantic relationship behaviour includes prosocial behaviour such as openness, positivity, assurance, social networks, shared tasks and conflict management whereas negative romantic relationship behaviour include antisocialbehaviours such as jealousy induction, avoidance, destructive conflict, allowing control, spying and infidelity.

Positive Romantic Relationship Maintenance Behaviours-

Video Calling or face timing is a positive romantic relationship maintenance behaviour. Amount of face-to-face interaction can prove to be a distinguishing factor between happy and not so happy long distance relationships, with individuals who have periodic face-to-face interaction using more maintenance and experience greater satisfaction and commitment than individuals in long distance relationships, with no face-to-face interaction (Dainton & Aylor, 2002).

Stafford and Canary(1991), who identified five maintenance behaviours. Positivity is defined as behavior that is cheerful and optimistic; openness is described as self-disclosure; assurancesare expressions of love and commitment; social networks are relying on commonfriends; and sharing tasks is sharing in equal responsibility within the relationship(Stafford & Canary, 1991).

Savouring can save relationships too. But what is savouring?

Savouring is the act of focusing on, enhancing, and extending the pleasant feelings associated with events.

Individuals might enjoy experiences that are currently taking place in the natural world (concurrent savouring), memories of past events that have already happened (retrospective savouring) or even experiences they want to have in the future (prospective savouring). Savouring, as a technique for emotion control, can help people see things from a different angle and develop understanding of their issues (Bryant & Veroff. 2017).

In fact, individuals who savour report happier emotions and lower levels of neuroticism, anhedonia and hopelessness. Additionally, savouring improves mood and sadness (Hurley & Kwon, 2013) and promotes happiness and acts as a positive romantic relationship maintenance behaviour (Quoidbach et al., 2009).

The role of communication cannot be stressed enough as a relationship maintenance behaviour. A strong and happy romantic relationship is built on effective communication. It is an essential instrument for preserving mutual understanding, trust and emotional closeness. Open, sincere and polite communication promotes intimacy and fortifies the bond between people. Partners that communicate well are able to honestly and effectively convey their needs, wants and views. Couples who communicate well are able to resolve issues amicably by voicing their concerns without placing blame or judgmenton one another.

In a relationship, open and honest communication fosters trust and a feeling of emotional safety. The bond between couples grows stronger and the foundation of trust is reinforced when they feel at ease opening up to one another about their feelings, worries and vulnerabilities. Clear communication reduces the possibility of miscommunications and misunderstandings, which can fuel animosity or hostility.

Partners may prevent misunderstandings and guarantee that their needs are acknowledged by communicating their intentions, wants and boundaries in a clear and concise manner.

Cultivating emotional intimacy and connection in relationships hinges on substantive dialogue. Couples fortify their bond and nurture a sense of closeness by engaging in open discussions about their emotions, aspirations and thoughts. Within a relationship, effective communication serves as a catalyst for personal growth. By conversing about ambitions, offering constructive feedback and expressing encouragement, partners can support each other's individual and collective development (Nicholson, 2020).

In romantic relationships, certain behaviours are paramount for maintaining and enhancing the emotional connection. These include expressing gratitude, offering compliments and demonstrating physical affection. The consistent acknowledgement of each other's contributions, regardless of their magnitude, fosters a sense of recognition and validation between partners (Gordon et al., 2012). Mutual praise cultivates a nurturing and affirming atmosphere within the relationship while simultaneously bolstering self-esteem and reinforcing positive attributes and behaviours. Moreover, physical expressions of affection, such as embracing and cuddling, trigger the release of oxytocin, often referred to as the "bonding hormone," which intensifies feelings of intimacy and attachment (Burke & Young, 2012).

A key component of relationship maintenance is self-efficacy or the conviction that one can successfully lead and control their romantic relationship. When people have strong self-efficacy in their relationships, they engage in ways that actively support the well-being and longevity of their union. These actions are necessary to develop intimacy, mutual understanding and the ability to overcome obstacles as a team. Proactive problem-solving and conflict resolution are traits of people who have high self-efficacy in romantic relationships. They approach problems with confidence, working together with their partner and using good communication techniques to discover solutions that satisfy both of them.

Research indicates that individuals who perceive themselves as more adept relationship partners report higher engagement in five key relationship maintaining behaviours: positivity, openness, assurances, network integration and task sharing. These relationship-promoting behaviours encompass a range of actions: positivity refers to cheerful and optimistic conduct; openness involves self-disclosure; assurances are expressions of love and commitment; social network integration entails reliance on mutual friends; and task sharing denotes equal distribution of responsibilities within the relationship. These behaviours, in turn, correlate with enhanced relationship satisfaction. Notably, beyond this mediated relationship, a direct link between self-efficacy and satisfaction has also been observed (Weiser & Weigel, 2016).

Subsequent refinements to this framework introduced two additional behaviours: advice-giving, which involves expressing thoughts and feelings about one's partner directly to them, and conflict management, which refers to the use of integrative strategies during disagreements. Intriguingly, while these behaviours are generally considered "positive," research has also suggested that certain behaviours perceived as "negative" may play a role in relationship maintenance, highlighting the complex dynamics of interpersonal interactions.

Negative Romantic Relationship Maintenance Behaviours-

Research in relationship dynamics has revealed that seemingly negative behaviours can paradoxically serve to maintain romantic relationships. Ayres (1983) identified avoidance as a tactic employed to preserve relationships. Expanding on this, Dindia and Baxter (1987) categorised maintenance behaviours into 11 groups, including "antisocial strategies" which encompassed actions like fighting, issuing threats or ultimatums and displaying negative behaviours such as coldness, insolence, arrogance or breaking contact.

Intriguingly, even deception has been found to play a role in relationship maintenance. Buller and Burgoon (1999) posited that lying can reduce the likelihood of confrontation, thereby fostering more harmonious relationships (Cole, 2001). This aligns with Metts' (1989) finding that one of the primary motivations for lying in romantic relationships is to sustain the connection. Similarly, expressions of jealousy may serve a maintenance function, with Guerrero and Andersen (1998) suggesting that preserving relationships is a key driver of jealous behaviour.

Further refining this concept, Dainton and Gross (2008) developed a measure of negative relational maintenance behaviours. They identified six behaviours commonly perceived as negative yet serving maintenance functions: allowing control, engaging in destructive conflict, spying, inducing jealousy, practicing avoidance and infidelity.

The concept of 'allowing control' in relationships presents a complex dynamic. This behaviour, characterised by an intense focus on one's partner to the exclusion of other relationships or responsibilities, can be interpreted in various ways. In the context of passionate love, it might manifest as a relatively benign desire for constant togetherness. However, it can also take on a more sinister form in abusive relationships, where isolation becomes a tool for maintaining control over the victim.

Jealousy and distrust, often considered negative emotions, can paradoxically serve as forms of relationship maintenance. Research by Dainton and Stokes (2015) indicates that jealousy induction, deliberately provoking jealousy in one's partner, is a recognized maintenance strategy. Interestingly, the manifestation of jealousy differs between genders: men typically express it through anger or violence, while women more often display sadness or depression.

Contrary to conventional wisdom, destructive conflict in romantic relationships can temporarily heighten desire. The intensity of emotionally charged conflicts often elicits strong reactions, inadvertently increasing both partners' emotional engagement. This heightened state can prompt reevaluation of feelings and the relationship's value, potentially rekindling desire to resolve issues and restore balance. The conflict's emotional arousal may create a sense of urgency and passion, drawing partners closer in their efforts to overcome challenges and rejuvenate their connection.

Technology has become an integral part of relationship dynamics in the digital age, particularly among younger generations. While it facilitates connection, it has also enabled negative behaviours such as cyber stalking – the unauthorized monitoring of romantic partners (Marcum et al., 2017). Spying, which includes checking a partner's social media and phone without consent, is classified as a negative maintenance behaviour that undermines the fundamental pillars of a healthy relationship: mutual respect, trust and privacy.

Paradoxically, avoidance in romantic relationships can sometimes increase attraction. When one partner withdraws or creates distance, it can spark curiosity and desire in the other. This behaviour introduces uncertainty, prompting the partner to seek validation and reassurance, potentially out of fear of losing the connection or a desire to mend what appears to be fraying. However, while this strategy might temporarily pique interest, persistent avoidance can ultimately erode relationship security and trust leading to dissatisfaction and potential dissolution.

Perhaps most controversially, infidelity has been identified as a negative maintenance behaviour. While it may seem counterintuitive that such a culturally reviled act could serve a maintenance function, especially given its status as a leading cause of divorce (Buunk & Dijkstra, 2006), research has uncovered some unexpected findings. Buunk et al. (2018) found that individuals who engaged in extra-dyadic relationships reported certain perceived benefits, including personal growth and enhanced self-esteem. This suggests that even behaviours widely considered detrimental to relationships can, in some instances, be viewed by participants as serving a maintenance function, although in a highly problematic and potentially destructive manner.

Even more counter-intuitively it was found that perpetrators of relational transgressions often believe that their primary relationship has improved as a result of the affair. Interestingly, research indicates that the most common reasons for infidelity focus on the attractions of the extra-dyadic relationship rather than on problems with the primary relationship. As such, engaging in infidelity may be perceived as a way to maintain a relationship by providing rewards not found in the primary relationship (Dainton & Gross, 2008).

Research has illuminated the intricate relationship between attachment styles and relational maintenance behaviours. Goodboy and Bolkan (2011) found that individuals with secure attachment are less likely to engage in negative relational maintenance behaviours. Conversely, those with dismissive or fearful-avoidant attachment styles show a higher propensity for employing specificnegative maintenance strategies. This aligns with findings from Goodboy et al. (2010), which indicate that negative maintenance behaviours are more prevalent in relationships characterisedby low quality.

In the contemporary digital landscape, the dynamics of romantic relationships have evolved beyond traditional face-to-face interactions. Social media platforms have emerged as crucial tools for couples to nurture their connections, express affection and strengthen their bonds. These digital spaces offer novel avenues for partners to foster love and intimacy, complementing in-person interactions with continuous online engagement. As such, the maintenance of romantic relationships in the digital age has expanded to encompass a blend of physical and virtual expressions of care and commitment, reflecting the changing nature of modern love and connection.

Couples can use social media to show their love and commitment by tagging one other in heartfelt posts, sending love notes publicly and posting images together. Through these acts, they affirm their relationship and demonstrate to the outside world how deeply they are connected. Additionally, social media platforms give couples the chance to communicate virtually or in person throughout the day by likingng, commenting on or texting each other's postings.

A comprehensive study by Stewart et al. (2014) explored the interplay between relationship dynamics and Facebook usage. The findings revealed nuanced patterns of relational maintenance behaviours on the platform. When partners perceived uncertainty in their relationship's status or definition, they tended to engage in more Facebook monitoring. Conversely, those who felt confident about their relationship's future and definition were likelier to use the platform for assurances and open communication. Interestingly, Facebook jealousy correlated with increased use of positive interactions, openness, assurances and monitoring on the platform. Partners who reported high relationship satisfaction demonstrated more positive interactions and assurances on Facebook.

Complementing these findings, Dainton & Berkoski (2013) observed that online partner monitoring showed a moderate association with emotional jealousy. Their research emphasizes that the impact of Facebook on romantic relationships is less about the quantity of time spent on the platform and more about how it is utilized.

During arguments in romantic relationships, aggressive humor is employed as a negative relational maintenance strategy. In order to release emotional concerns regarding the status of their relationship while maintaining it, romantic partners may engage in such humor. When faced with disagreement, people are driven to cover up topics of conversation, get their partners to respond and defuse tension by using aggressive humor. Sarcasm, mimicry and repetition are used to create aggressive humor (Anderson & DiTunnariello, 2016).

To sum up, the foundation of happy and healthy relationships is the maintenance of romantic relationships. These actions, whether constructive or destructive, have a significant effect on the dynamics, contentment and durability of relationships. Couples can build intimacy, mutual respect and trust by regularly practicing positive maintenance behaviours like communication, support and appreciation. This will help to fortify their relationship.

On the other hand, conflict avoidance and relationship health depend heavily on addressing and reducing negative maintenance behaviour, such neglect or criticism. Ultimately, couples can overcome obstacles, strengthen their bond and create a strong and long-lasting relationship based on love and understanding by putting an emphasis on positive maintenance behaviour whileaddressing bad ones.

Aggressive humor during arguments serves as another negative maintenance strategy. Partners may employ sarcasm, mimicry, and repetition to address relationship concerns while maintaining the connection (Anderson & DiTunnariello, 2016). This sheds light on the "dark side" of relationship maintenance and contributes to our understanding of potentially harmful behaviours within romantic partnerships.

Ultimately, successful relationships require a balance of positive maintenance behaviours to build intimacy and trust, while addressing and minimizing negative behaviours that can erode relationship health. By focusing on constructive strategies and managing destructive ones, couples can navigate challenges and foster enduring, loving relationships.

CHAPTER – 15

Extra Dyadic Interactions

Extradyadic relations encompass sexual or emotional infidelity that occurs outside the agreed-upon boundaries of a committed relationship. This term applies broadly to instances of unfaithfulness, regardless of whether the partners are married or not. While commonly referred to as "cheating" in casual conversation, the phenomenon is also known in more formal contexts as extra-dyadic infidelity, non-consensual non-monogamy or simply extramarital affairs.

It's crucial to distinguish that in the case of open relationships, where partners have explicitly agreed to allow outside sexual encounters, such activities are not considered extradyadic or unfaithful. The concept fundamentally hinges on the violation of trust and the breach of established relationship agreements, rather than the specific nature of the external involvement.

Because infidelity is considered a severe relationship transgression that often predicts relationship dissolution/divorce (Tsapelas et al.,2011), the bulk of prior research in psychology, communication and family studies posits that infidelity stems primarily from suboptimal relationship experiences such as feeling neglected by a partner or spouse (Barta & Kiene, 2005), though some work suggests that infidelity is both a cause and consequence of poor relationship health (Previti & Amato, 2004).

Evolutionary theories propose that infidelity, despite its inherent risks, may have evolved as an adaptive strategy to enhance reproductive success or secure new partners. This ancestral predisposition potentially explains the prevalence of intense jealousy, mate-guarding behaviours and efforts to prevent infidelity in exclusive relationships (Buss, 2018). According to these models, there may be sex-specific motivations for extradyadic relations. Men, given their lower biological investment in offspring, might be more inclined to maximise their number of sexual partners. Women, on the other hand, might benefit from a dual strategy: securing genetic advantages through affairs while maintaining access to resources and stability through a primary partner (Schmitt & Jonason, 2015).

Infidelity is influenced by a complex interplay of factors, including individual characteristics and social contexts. Access to potential partners plays a crucial role, shaped by personal attributes like income and urban living as well as social factors such as cultural attitudes towards affairs and the presence of interested individuals (Allen et al., 2005). Despite these varied influences, most theoretical models characteriseinfidelity as a significant breach of trust and commitment within a relationship, acknowledging its potential for negative impacts on both individuals and couples.

Research has revealed that the motivations behind infidelity can significantly influence its nature and outcomes. Affairs driven by relationship-specific factors such as anger towards a partner or a lack of love, tend to be more prolonged and public, often leading to the dissolution of the primary relationship. In contrast, infidelity motivated by situational factors like stress or intoxication, typically results in briefer, less satisfying encounters. These situationally-motivated affairs are less likely to be disclosed to the primary partner and less frequently lead to relationship termination (Selterman, et al., 2021).

The tendency to focus on attractive alternative partners while in an established relationship can lead to detrimental outcomes including infidelity and relationship breakdown. However, the degree to which individuals notice and remember potential alternatives is influenced by various relational factors. Research indicates that love for one's partner is associated with reduced visual attention to images of attractive alternatives. Additionally, love, commitment and the degree of self-expansion experienced within the relationship all correlate with reported attention to alternatives.

Interestingly, an individual's need for self-expansion appears to play a unique role. While it doesn't necessarily predict increased attention to alternatives, it does correlate with enhanced memory for potential partners who possess self-expansion-promoting qualities that differ from those of the current partner. This suggests that individuals may unconsciously retain information about alternatives that could potentially fulfil unmet needs for personal growth and development within their current relationship.

Duration of the relationship also plays a role in infidelity. Among married women, the likelihood of extramarital involvement peaks in the seventh year of marriage, then declines; but among married men, the likelihood of extramarital involvement decreases over time until the eighteenth year of matrimony, after which the likelihood of extramarital involvement increases (Liu, 2000).

Allen and colleagues (2008) found strong and consistent effects of communication patterns: couples who experienced sexual infidelity in the first year of marriage indicated more problematic communication before marriage such as lower levels of positive interaction and higher levels of negative and invalidating interaction. According to the investment model (Rusbult, 1980), commitment (a psychological attachment and a motivation to continue a relationship) is the leadingforce in maintaining romantic relationships.

Factors that influence commitment include satisfaction (how happy the individual is with the relationship), alternative quality (potential satisfaction provided outside the relationship such as dating another person, being alone, etc.) and investments (things the individual would lose if the relationship ends such as shared possessions, friends, etc.). Individuals who are highly committed may be less likely to engage in infidelity because they are motivated to derogate potential alternative partners in order to protect the relationship and consider the long-term ramifications of infidelity when tempted.

Factors affecting EDI

- Relationship infidelities are motivated by many distinct factors, indicating motivations of dissatisfaction, neglect, anger and sexual desire (Barta & Kiene, 2005).

- Factors including lack of love ("I had 'fallen out of love with' my primary partner"), low commitment ("I was not very committed to my primary partner"), esteem ("I wanted to enhance my popularity"), gaining sexual variety ("I wanted a greater variety of sexual partners"), and situational factors ("I was drunk and not thinking clearly").

- Psychological factors also play a significant role. Attachment insecurity has been linked to motivations stemming from anger, lack of love, neglect, low commitment, and esteem-seeking behaviour. Individuals with an unrestricted sociosexual orientation tend to be more motivated by the desire for sexual variety. Additionally, implicit beliefs about relationships - such as views on personal growth, destiny, and romanticism - correlate differentially with motivations like sexual desire, low commitment, lack of love, and feelings of neglect(Selterman et al., 2019).

- **Role of gender-** Research on extradyadic sex has revealed several factors that can explain in part why people are sometimes inclined to (and ultimately do) engage in extradyadic sex. First, research found biological sex differences in extradyadic involvements showing that men in heterosexual relationships are more likely to engage in extradyadic sex than women (Frisco et al., 2017).

Research on gender differences in extradyadic behaviour reveals consistent patterns across various aspects of infidelity. Men, in comparison to women, exhibit a stronger inclination towards sexual infidelity and are more likely to act on these desires. They tend to have a higher number of sexual partners outside their primary relationships and engage in more frequent episodes of infidelity, ranging from one-night stands to long-term affairs(Brand et al., 2007).

When men do engage in extradyadic relationships, they are more likely to pursue physical intimacy, including sexual intercourse, with their affair partners. Interestingly, despite this higher level of physical involvement, men are less prone to developing emotional attachments or falling in love with their extradyadic partners (Allen et al., 2008).

The motivations driving male infidelity also differ from those of women. Men more frequently cite sexual reasons as the primary motivation for their extradyadic behaviour (Barta & Kiene, 2005). This aligns with broader patterns of male sexuality, which often emphasise physical gratification over emotional connection in contexts outside of committed relationships (Glass & Wright, 1985).

Women, in contrast to men, tend to form stronger emotional connections with their extradyadic partners. Their motivations for engaging in infidelity often stem from a desire for intimacy and enhanced self-esteem, rather than primarily sexual gratification (Spanier & Margolis, 1983).

Women who engage in extradyadic relationships frequently report feelings of cognitive dissonance, expressing that such behaviour feels uncharacteristic of their typical selves. They also demonstrate greater concern about potential social repercussions, particularly regarding negative judgments from others(Brand et al., 2007).

A notable distinction lies in how the primary relationship's quality influences extradyadic behaviour across genders. For women, the strength of extradyadic sexual desires and the frequency of affairs correlatesstrongly with the level of reciprocity in their primary relationship. This suggests that women's inclination towards infidelity is more closely tied to their satisfaction within their existing partnership (Prins & colleagues, 1993).

In contrast, men's propensity for infidelity appears to be somewhat independent of their primary relationship's status. This indicates that men may pursue extradyadic relationships regardless of their satisfaction levels within their current partnership, pointing to potentially different underlying motivations or triggers for infidelity between genders.

Research consistently demonstrates a negative correlation between relationship satisfaction, sexual satisfaction and the likelihood of engaging in extradyadic sexual behaviour (Mark et al., 2011).

Fincham and May (2017) identified overall relationship satisfaction, sexual satisfaction and the degree of love and affection as among the most reliable predictors of extradyadic involvement.

A systematic review by Haseli et al. (2019) proposed that various sexuality-related factors play a significant role in the psychological processes underlying extradyadic behaviours. Specifically, they hypothesised that characteristics such as sexual desire, sexual interest and sexual excitement influence an individual's propensity to engage in infidelity.

These findings collectively underscore the complex interplay between relationship quality, sexual dynamics and the likelihood of extradyadic involvement. Research suggests that maintaining high levels of relationship and sexual satisfaction may serve as a protective factor against infidelity, while also highlighting the importance of understanding individual sexual characteristics in predicting extradyadic behaviour.

Men who eventually engage in sexual infidelity tend to report lower levels of relationship satisfaction even before official start of relationship, suggesting a pre-existing discontent. In contrast, women who later commit infidelity do not typically indicate lower pre-relationship satisfaction levels. This disparity points to potentially different trajectories in developing romantic dissatisfaction between genders. For women, the process appears to be more gradual, characterised by what could be termed a "disillusionment process." Initially, they may overlook or downplay early relationship shortcomings. However, these unaddressed issues can accumulate over time, gradually eroding satisfaction and potentially increasing the likelihood of infidelity as the relationship progresses (Allen et al., 2008).

- **Big Five personality traits** -Certain personality traits have been linked to an increased propensity for engaging in extradyadic relationships. Individuals scoring high in extraversion may be more likely to pursue affairs, potentially enhancing their leverage within their primary sexual partnership. Additionally, low agreeableness, high neuroticism, low conscientiousness and elevated psychoticism are associated with a greater tendency towards infidelity.

Research by Mark et al. (2011) indicates that for both sexes, a perceived mismatch in sexual attitudes and values between partners correlates with a higher likelihood of seeking extra dyadic encounters. These findings suggest that personality factors and sexual compatibility play significant roles in relationship fidelity.

- Individuals with insecure attachment styles, specifically those with high levels of anxiety or avoidance are more likely to engage in infidelity (Ghiasi et al., 2024). Attachment avoidance has been positively associated with extradyadic sex (Beaulieu-Pelletier et al., 2011).It was found that individuals high in attachment avoidance (compared to those low in attachment avoidance) experienced relatively lower romantic attraction in interactions with current partners and greater romantic attraction when interacting with potential alternatives (Overall & Sibley, 2008).
- Another factor that has received much attention in relation to extradyadic interaction is an unrestricted sociosexual orientation which has been associated with past extradyadic sexual involvements and a greater willingness to engage in extradyadic behaviours (Mattingly et al., 2011).

Sociosexuality, sometimes called sociosexual orientation, is the individual difference in the willingness to engage in sexual activity outside of a committed relationship. Individuals who are more restricted sociosexually are less willing to engage in casual sex; they prefer greater love, commitment and emotional closeness before having sex with romantic partners. Individuals who have been betrayed in the past tend to report more unrestricted sociosexuality. More precisely, people who have experienced betrayal by their partner typically experience increased sexual desire and a reduced sense of worth in their romantic relationship (Arantes et al., 2020).

- The rise in popularity of the Internet has led to an ever-increasing number of people meeting partners, outside of their relationship.Many of these relationships start off innocently and end after a short period of time. However, an alarming number develop into emotional and/or physical extra dyadic affairs. This phenomenon is referred to as Internet infidelity. We define Internet infidelity as using the Internet to take sexual energy of any sort–thoughts, feelings and behaviours–outside of a committed sexual relationship in such a way that it damages the relationship.

Internet infidelity is a complex issue, a multifaceted phenomenon that includes both an emotional, sexual (Abdi et al., 2012) and communicative component.

Justifications behindInternet infidelity can be grouped into several categories of intrapersonal factors (sensation-seeking, low self-esteem and negative self-image and suppressed excitement), conflicts (unfulfilled emotional needs, instability and difference in couple's values, lack of attention to boundaries, discord, revenge on the partner and unattractive partner) and sexual reasons (curiosity for sexual experiences, sexual experiences before commencement of relationship and sexual frustration) (Roman, 2020).

- Religiosity has also been found to be a predictor, or correlate, of infidelity. Infidelity has consistently been reported more often by individuals who endorse no religious affiliation than by those who do (Mattingly et al., 2010).

- Several studies have found that education is associated with infidelity, in that highly educated persons are more likely to report engaging in infidelity than less educated individuals (Atkins et al., 2001).
- Income has been found to be related to infidelity. Individuals with higher incomes are more prone to engage in infidelity and this may be because their professional and personal lives include more opportunities to engage in extradyadic relations (Allen et al., 2005).

Types of EDI

Physical/ Sexual Infidelity- Physical or sexual infidelity is widely recognised as a form of cheating, involving intimate physical contact with someone outside the primary romantic relationship. Research by Beltrán-Morillas et al. (2019) indicates that sexual extra dyadic behaviours are generally perceived as more detrimental and hurtful than emotional transgressions. However, the precise definition of infidelity can vary considerably between relationships, as it is fundamentally dependent on the boundaries and agreements established by the partners involved. The spectrum of physical infidelity is broad, potentially encompassing acts ranging from kissing to sexual intercourse. This complexity underscores the importance of clear communication and mutual understanding within relationships regarding what constitutes a breach of trust.

Viewing porn as a case of physical infidelity?

Some couples might consider viewing pornography to be harmless, even a typical form of sexual expression that has no detrimental effects on their relationship. Since there is no immediate contact with another person, they view it as a private activity that does not correspond to physical infidelity. On the other hand, some individuals could perceive the viewing of pornography as a betrayal or a breach of trust, notably when it deviates from the mutually agreed-upon standards and guidelines.

They would contend that it can lead to emotional detachment, irrational expectations or discontent in the relationship, which would then have an indirect effect on the closeness of the couple on both a physical and emotional level. Ultimately, the mutual understanding and boundaries established by the people in the relationship will determine whether or not watching pornography is regarded as physical infidelity.

The classification of pornography use as a form of infidelity remains a subject of debate. From a psychological perspective consuming pornographic material does not constitute a genuine sexual interaction, as it lacks the element of shared activity between two or more individuals. This view emphasizes the absence of 'real interaction' between the viewer and the subjects depicted in pornographic content. Proponents of this stance argue that private pornography use does not involve actual sexual intercourse and can instead be categorized as a form of sexual fantasizing. Drawing on Woollard's (2010) distinction, this argument highlights the fundamental difference between imagining a sexual encounter and engaging in one. Thus, from this viewpoint, pornography consumption is more closely aligned with fantasy than with physical infidelity, potentially placing it in a different ethical category within the context of relationship boundaries.

Online Adult Chat Rooms a case of physical Infidelity?

Online personal erotic interactions, such as the use of adult chat rooms are a form of infidelity. Using an online chat room might feel like a serious betrayal of trust and affection. This is due to the fact that these kinds of conscious contacts frequently entail some degree of emotional and sexual intimacy with a person who is not a partner, which may compromise the emotional and sexual exclusivity that is anticipated in a partnership.

Such interactions, especially when they involve masturbation, contain many of the 'basic characteristics of actual sex like excitement, anticipation, satisfaction and orgasm' (Ben-Ze'ev, 2004). It also involves a person one is exclusively interacting with.

Emotional Infidelity-

An emotional affair may be developing when a person begins to conceal personal information from their primary partner and confides in someone else they feel more emotionally attracted to and intimate with about their innermost feelings and thoughts. Emotional infidelity includes the development of deep, intimate feelings for an extradyadic partner. Emotional infidelity includes the development of deep, intimate feelings for an extra dyadic partner.

Women saw emotional infidelity as carrying the potential of later sexual betrayal in such partnerships. This suggests that the nuances involved with conceptualising emotional infidelity may surpass the conditions needed to fulfill sexual infidelity.

Women perceived emotional infidelity as more upsetting than men did and the explanation provided by them was that women believe that men are not able to maintain sexual faithfulness in their relationships, but will still remain emotionally loyal to their partners regardless.

Men appear to hold more permissive attitudes towards physical infidelity than women do. But contrary, in terms of reaction, men also reported experiencing greater levels of stress related to the sexual infidelity of their partner, whereas women react more negatively to emotional infidelity than men. However, women also seem to consider more behaviours as infidelity compared to men in both offline and online spaces (Rokach & Chan, 2023).

It was found that men, when forced to decide, were more upset by sexual infidelity and women by emotional infidelity. It was also found that men were more likely to believe that women have sex when in love and that women believe that men have sex even when they are not in love (Whitty & Quigley, 2008).

Cyber infidelity

Cyber infidelity is a contemporary relationship dilemma that appears on social media sites and dating apps among other online venues. The boundaries between loyalty and betrayal can become hazy in the digital era, which can cause emotional distress and problems with trust. Having private online chats or developing close relationships with people who are not in a committed relationship is one aspect of cyber infidelity. Although these exchanges may begin innocuously, they have the potential to swiftly turn into emotional relationships in which partners devote their time, feelings and attention to someone other than their significant other.

Internet pornography is any content that presents graphic nudity online in an effort to increase arousal. Erotic videos on the internet that emphasize sensuality over sexuality can also be considered pornography. Emotional component is not the only thing that might be present in online sexual behaviours. These online behaviours might be carried out in public (webcam or live chat) or privately (masturbating and watching pornography). These actions may be regarded as acts of cyber infidelity if the person is already a romantic relationship (Carroll et al., 2008).

Gender-based stereotypes and group dynamics often influence perceptions of infidelity. Two contrasting theories emerge in this context. On one hand, culturally ingrained stereotypes about sexual behaviour may lead individuals to judge female transgressors more severely than their male counterparts. Conversely, intergroup bias theory as discussed by Hackathorn & Harvey (2011), suggests that people tend to evaluate out-group members or those of the opposite sex more harshly than in-group members or those of the same sex. This dichotomy highlights the complex interplay between societal norms, gender expectations and group affiliations in shaping attitudes towards infidelity. The tension between these perspectives underscores the multifaceted nature of moral judgments in the realm of sexual behaviour and relationships.

Micro Cheating:

In psychology, the term "micro-cheating" describes small acts or behaviours that could imply someone is emotionally or physically involved with someone outside of their committed relationship. Micro-cheating involves seemingly innocent behaviours that over time can destroy trust and intimacy, in contrast to traditional infidelity, which usually involves obvious breaches of trust such as physical closeness or emotional affairs. Excessive flirtation, clandestine communication with someone other than a partner, having a dating app profile, leaving a wedding ring while going outside, chatting with ex-partnersand preserving pictures or mementoes from previous relationships are a few examples of micro-cheatingbehaviours. Even though each of these behaviours might not appear serious on its own, when together, they may reveal a lack of dedication or emotional engagement in the main connection.

The psychological effects of micro cheating on people and their relationships can be profound. Micro cheating by one person might be a sign of underlying discontent or unfulfilled needs in the relationship, which can cause shame, uncertainty or conflict. When one partner sees these actions, it can cause feelings of betrayal, jealousy and insecurity in the other, which eventually ruins the intimacy and trust in the relationship.

Financial infidelity:

Financial infidelity can significantly strain relationships, manifesting as deception regarding income, earnings methods, debt, spending habits or undisclosed assets. Research by Garbinsky et al. (2020) highlights various forms this deception may take, including hidden cash reserves or secret bank accounts. The impact of such behaviour is substantial; Jeanfreau et al. (2018) found that individuals who experienced financial infidelity reported lower marital and life satisfaction compared to those who had not. Interestingly, more organised individuals were less prone to keeping financial secrets from their partners.

The interplay between economic roles and infidelity reveals complex gender dynamics. Munsch (2015) observed that breadwinning status affects men and women differently: for men, it increases the likelihood of infidelity while for women it decreases it. This disparity may be attributed to women's efforts to mitigate perceived gender norm violations and preserve potentially strained relationships through fidelity. Economic dependency, however, increases the probability of infidelity for both genders with a more pronounced effect on men.

High Risk Professions

Owing to elements like work-related stress, long periods spent away from home, frequent travel or an atmosphere that encourages close, intense relationships, some occupations are sometimes thought to have greater rates of infidelity. Because of the nature of their jobs and the attention they get, those in the entertainment business such as actors and musicians are frequently tempted. Similar to this, professions requiring a lot of travel, like those of pilots, flight attendants and corporate executives, may present chances for adultery because of extended times spent apart from their partners. It is well known that certain corporate work settings can be ruthless and unforgiving, encouraging "a whatever-it-takes approach" to finish tasks assigned and achieve objectives.

People in high-stress occupations like law or medical may look for solace and affirmation outside of their primary connection.

Furthermore, occupations like law enforcement or the military that require close collaboration with others in demanding settings can occasionally create deep relationships. The conditions surrounding far-flung deployment may make cheating more appealing and reduce the likelihood of being discovered.

The challenges of long-distance relationships often persist even after partners reunite. Extended periods of separation can lead to unmet needs and significant relationship deficits, potentially increasing the likelihood of infidelity. This vulnerability doesn't necessarily dissipate upon reunification, as the strain of prolonged distance may have lasting effects on the relationship's dynamic.

Recent trends indicate a rise in infidelity cases where individuals seek emotional or psychological support outside their primary relationship. Rosaline & Kasaraneni (2024) suggest that the repercussions of extradyadic affairs may be particularly severe for those engaging in infidelity while working from home. This scenario presents a unique set of circumstances where the boundaries between personal and professional life blur, potentially exacerbating the impact of infidelity on the relationship. This increased proximity to home and family while simultaneously engaging in clandestine behaviour may intensify feelings of guilt, conflict and overall strain the relationship.

However, it is important to remember that infidelity is a personal decision that is not exclusively influenced by one's line of work.

Open Marriages/ Open Relationships

Having multiple romantic or sexual partners at the same time is known as an open relationship. Both parties acknowledge that the arrangement is neither monogamous nor exclusive. The commitment part of the arrangement is crucial since one or both partners participate in romantic or sexual activities outside of the relationship.

Research by Selterman et al. (2023) reveals intriguing dynamics within consensually open relationships. In these partnerships, the traditional correlation between low relationship quality and infidelity appears to be significantly diminished. Individuals in open relationships who engaged in extradyadic affairs did not typically report decreased satisfaction, love or commitment in their primary relationships. Moreover, these affairs did not predict a decline in relationship quality over time, as is often observed in monogamous partnerships.

The study suggests that for individuals proactively seeking affairs within the context of open relationships, poor dyadic or marital relationships were not primary motivators. Notably, these extra dyadic encounters did not seem to exert a strong negative impact on the primary relationships. Additionally, personal ethics played a less significant role in shaping individuals' attitudes towards their affairs in these consensual non-monogamous arrangements.

Positive Effects of Extra dyadic Interactions

While extra dyadic relationships are generally viewed negatively due to their potential to harm trust and emotional bonds in relationships, there is some research that proves there can be positive effects in certain contexts. These potential benefits are highly controversial and depend on the specific dynamics and agreements within a relationship. Here are a few perspectives that you might find interesting:

Personal Growth and Self-Discovery: Stable relationships sometimes create monotony. Not only the partner but an individual can also get accustomed to seeing things through one lens. Engaging in an extra dyadic relationship can sometimes lead individuals to a deeper understanding of their own desires, needs and identity. This self-discovery might prompt an individual to address unfulfilled aspects of their primary relationship or personal life.

Renewed Appreciation for the Primary Relationship: Paradoxically, some individuals may find that an affair makes them appreciate their primary relationship more. The contrast between the stability and emotional depth of their relationship and the novelty of an affair can highlight the unique value of their long-term partnership. An individual might get more breathing space which can prove a miracle for primary relationships. Secondly, an individual also starts being more forgiving and tolerant of the primary partner's annoying habits because one realizes that no one is perfect and there is also cheaters guilt that makes an individual more forgiving.

Resolving Unmet demands: Sometimes, unfulfilled emotional or sexual demands from the primary relationship might be addressed in an extra dyadic connection. Also, the new affair has no emotional baggage of the past. Initially there is a lot of romanticism and charm which creates an atmosphere of relaxation. This can occasionally result in a more contented and balanced existence for the person, but it frequently comes at the expense of openness and confidence in their main connection.

Catalyst for Change: Discovering or engaging in an affair can serve as a wake-up call for couples to address underlying issues in their relationship. It might lead to open conversations about needs, desires and changes necessary for a healthier relationship dynamic.

It increases self-confidence and makes one happier

Chances of experiencing boring dull and dry days increase with the length of the relationship. There is a lack of communication, appreciation, new shared activities and sexual activity. Life gets even more boring when you give up on trying to look good or charm the partner. Having an affair might rekindle the desire to improve oneself. There is added newness to the routine. Self-improvement doesn't seem like a task anymore.

New relationshipsrelease feel-good hormones. Flowers are prettier, songs make more sense and an individual starts looking after oneself. One looks good, one feels better andknowsthat someone out there thinks about them, which is obviously a pleasant thought. Without a doubt, the sexual satisfaction and in some cases, the emotional intimacy one experiences can end up making one feel more satisfied in life. An individual turns livelier. Due to enthusiasm and feelings of affection, health hazards are reduced.

Reduction in stress and Reduced Health Hazards

Due to more initial communication and expression of concern, stress evaporates from life. Isolation and loneliness takes a back seat and individualsstartfeeling healthier (Sonali Singh et al., 2009).

Enhanced Creativity and Energy: The excitement and novelty of an extradyadic relationship can sometimes infuse individuals with renewed energy and creativity, which they might channel into other areas of their lives, including work and personal interests.

Negative Effect of Extra dyadic Interactions-

Extra dyadic interactions cause a lot of stress in the primary relationship. Individuals and their primary relationships may suffer greatly from extradyadic relationships. The most immediate effect is frequently a loss of trust, which can cause the deceived partner to feel deeply betrayed and emotionally hurt. Regaining this lost trust can be difficult and frequently results in long-term harm to the emotional connection between partners. Furthermore, learning of an affair can cause partners to experience severe emotions including despair, rage and insecurity, which can lower their emotional health and self-worth.

Knowing they are lying to their partner, the individual in the adulterous connection may also feel guilty, stressed and anxious. Anxiety and despair as well as a general decline in life satisfaction might result from this internal conflict. The foundation of the primary relationship may be further undermined by the pervasive climate of dishonesty and manipulation that can result from the secrecy and deception required to continue an affair.

Some of the issues that arise out of such relationships include the following-

Breach of Trust: The most immediate and often most devastating consequence is the breach of trust. Infidelity can shatter the foundation of trust that a relationship is built upon, making it extremely difficult to rebuild and causing long-term damage to the emotional bond between partners.

Psychological Pain: Specifically, these extra dyadic behaviours can have serious consequences, such as low self-esteem, mental problems, loss of trust, decreased personal and sexual confidence, rage, and guilt and in many cases leads to spousal battering and divorce (Russell et al., 2013).

Relationship Breakdown: Discovering an affair can lead to serious conflicts, estrangement and in many cases, separation or divorce. The breakdown of the primary relationship can have lasting repercussions on both partners, affecting their ability to form healthy relationships in the future.

Impact on Children: If children are involved, the negative effects of infidelity can extend to them as well. The resulting conflicts and potential separation can create a stressful and unstable environment, impacting their emotional and psychological development.

Social and Family Strain: Infidelity can strain relationships with extended family and friends, as these individuals may take sides or feel uncomfortable around the couple. This can lead to a loss of social support and a sense of isolation for both partners.

Guilt and Anxiety: The person engaging in the extra dyadic relationship may experience significant guilt, stress and anxiety due to the deception and dishonesty involved.

This internal conflict can lead to decreased life satisfaction and mental health issues such as depression and anxiety. The betrayed partner suffers significant damage to their self-image, personal confidence or sexual confidence, feelings of abandonment, attacks on their sense of belonging, betrayals of trust, enraged feelings and/or a surge of justification to leave their partners (Charn & Parnass, 1995).

Dishonesty and Manipulation: Maintaining an affair often involves a web of lies and deceit, creating an atmosphere of dishonesty and manipulation. This can further erode the integrity of the primary relationship and contribute to a toxic relational environment.

Legal and Financial Consequences: In cases of divorce, infidelity can lead to complex legal battles and financial consequences. Division of assets, custody disputes and alimony can add additional stress and financial strain to the individuals involved.

Trauma: The partner who has been cheated often develops trauma regarding the experience. This trauma impacts all the subsequent relationships of that person's life.

Extra-dyadic connections present a complex landscape of potential outcomes, encompassing both positive and negative ramifications. On the positive side, these relationships may catalyze personal growth, self-discovery and even foster a renewed appreciation for one's primary partnership. They can serve as catalysts for necessary changes within a relationship, addressing unmet needs and potentially revitalizing stagnant dynamics.

However, the negative consequences of such connections are often profound and far-reaching. These may include severe breaches of trust, significant emotional distress, and strain on the primary relationship. The impact can extend beyond the immediate partnership, affecting children and broader social networks. The inherent dishonesty and secrecy typically associated with extra-dyadic relationships can generate an atmosphere of tension and guilt, poisoning the foundations of trust and intimacy within the primary relationship.

Ultimately, the multifaceted nature of extra-dyadic connections underscores the critical importance of open communication, mutual respect and well-defined boundaries in maintaining the integrity and health of the primary relationships. These elements serve as safeguards against the potential destructive effects of infidelity while fostering an environment conducive to addressing relationship challenges constructively.

CHAPTER – 16

What Makes You Attractive?

A complex interaction of psychological, social and biological elements leads to romantic attraction. Although various people are drawn to different qualities, there are some universal psychological components that frequently support romantic attraction. Investigating many facets of human nature and interpersonal dynamics is necessary to comprehend the intricacies of how people are drawn to one another in romantic relationships. Often we think about a list of qualities that we would like in our romantic partners. Psychologically, some elements have been listed through various studies that play a role in determining our romantic choices.

While individual preferences vary, many women share common expectations when seeking a partner. Generally, women are drawn to men who exhibit charm, wit, intelligence and the ability to foster positive emotions. These qualities often take precedence over specific traits like joke-telling prowess, though some women may prioritize genuine attentiveness over humor. For men, confidence tends to be the most appealing characteristic in a potential partner, alongside shared interests. The alignment of hobbies and passions can significantly enhance the enjoyment and connection in the early stages of a relationship, making it a key factor in attraction for many men.

Research indicates that high school students often interact more frequently with romantic partners than with family members or friends (Laursen & Williams 1997). Studies on adolescents suggest that reproductive maturation may be influenced by physical proximity to parents, with closeness potentially inhibiting maturation and distance accelerating it - a mechanism that could reduce inbreeding and enhance reproductive fitness. When it comes to partner preferences, adolescents typically seek intelligence, interpersonal skills and physical attractiveness in their ideal mates (Regan& Joshi, 2003). In heterosexual relationships, male adolescents tend to date partners close to their own age, while females often choose older partners. Additionally, there's a preference for dating partners who share similar demographic characteristics, such as race and ethnicity, highlighting the importance of homogeneity in adolescent romantic choices (Carver et al., 2003).

Contemporary research reveals a notable congruence between young adolescent partners in various social and psychological attributes including popularity, physical allure and manifestations of depressive symptoms(Furman & Simon, 2008). These findings challenge the notion that adolescent romantic relationships are merely transient or inconsequential. Instead, they underscore the pivotal role these early romantic experiences play in shaping the foundation upon which young adult romantic relationships are built. Such insights illuminate the developmental significance of adolescent romances positioning them as crucial stepping stones in the broader landscape of interpersonal relationship formation and maturation (Meier & Allen, 2009).

The realm of adult romantic preferences is as diverse as the individuals themselves encompassing a wide spectrum of desired attributes in potential partners. These preferences are not formed in isolation but are shaped by a complex interplay of cultural norms, societal expectations and personal experiences, while simultaneously reflecting one's own beliefs and aspirations. A fundamental principle in understanding interpersonal attraction is the similarity-attraction hypothesis (SAH), which posits that individuals are inherently drawn to those who share similar characteristics. This seemingly straightforward yet profound concept serves as a cornerstone for much of the research conducted in the fields of relationship dynamics and interpersonal attraction. The SAH highlights the human tendency to gravitate towards familiarity and resonance in romantic pursuits, offering insight into the intricate tapestry of adult relationship formation (Montoya & Horton, 2013).

Although various people are drawn to different qualities, there are some universal psychological components that frequently support romantic attraction:

Physical Attractiveness

There is no doubt that another really important characteristic is physical attractiveness in adults (Regan et al., 2000). It does not mean that each individual wants to date Aditya Roy Kapoor or Tripti Dimri, it just means that people want their minimum subjective beauty standards to be fulfilled. Although humour, personality and friendliness do receive preference over physical attractiveness in some individuals (Regan et al, 2000). But these traits only come into play once minimum beauty standards are met.

Physical attractiveness has important social consequences. For example, beauty is associated with upward economic mobility, especially for women. It has long been noted that there exists a 'What is beautiful is good' stereotype for research on physical attractiveness stereotypes, whereby attractive individuals are perceived to possess a variety of positive personality attributions(Langlois et al., 2000).

Self Disclosure

Doesn't a long conversation make you instantly feel connected? Some late night texting which leads to some secret sharing makes you think about the other person in a different light. Indeed the thing called self disclosure sometimes plays a cupid.

The manifestation of attraction towards a potential partner encompasses a multifaceted response, involving cognitive, affective, motivational and behavioural components. This attraction may be expressed through positive thoughts and beliefs, pleasant emotions, a desire for proximity and even subtle physical behaviours such as reduced interpersonal distance(Wurst et al., 2018).. Central to the development of meaningful relationships is the concept of self-disclosure, which posits that the gradual revelation of personal information is crucial for building trust and deepening intimacy. As one partner begins to share more intimate details about their thoughts, emotions and experiences, it often encourages reciprocal disclosure from the other. This mutual unveiling of one's authentic self creates a foundation of trust and understanding in romantic partnerships. The process of sharing thoughts, feelings and allowing a partner to witness one's true essence fosters a deeper connection, ultimately leading to greater relationship satisfaction and fulfilment. This dynamic interplay of vulnerability and acceptance underscores the importance of open communication and emotional transparency in cultivating robust, intimate relationships (Vittengl & Holt, 2000).

Attachment Pattern

Attachment theory posits that our early emotional bonds significantly shape our future relationships. This influential framework suggests that we are unconsciously drawn to individuals who mirror and reinforce our deeply held beliefs and expectations about care, trust, abandonment, dependence, support, intimacy and vulnerability. Essentially, we tend to gravitate towards partners who echo the relational patterns we experienced with our primary attachment figures.

John Bowlby, a pioneering psychologist in this field, expanded on this concept by identifying four primary attachment types. These four distinct attachment styles profoundly influence our approach to relationship dynamics, sexual attitudes and expectations of romantic intimacy. This nuanced understanding of attachment styles provides valuable insights into the psychological underpinnings of our romantic behaviours and preferences, offering a framework for comprehending the complex interplay between our past experiences and current relational patterns.

Secure Attachment Style

This is a dream style to have in a romantic partner. When their partner is in distress, adults with secure attachments voluntarily and excitingly offer help. They turn to their partner for help when they are experiencing stress. In an open and sincere relationship characterised by stable attachment, each person feels loved and independent of the other. Adults who are securely attached are self-assured in their relationships and let their partners go freely as they develop personally. For the individuals with this attachment style, distance does not mean an alarm clock, they are the ones who will never check their partner's phone, or doubt their best friends of the opposite gender. An absolute green flag!

Anxious Attachment Styles

25 missed calls, 100 messages on whatsapp and extreme emotional reactions on a little distance are the kind we will be discussing now. Adults with anxious attachment styles are different from those with secure attachment patterns in that they are emotionally hungry. They really do not understand the concept of space. Love bombing and making the other person guilty with their extreme love and attention is a regular ritual. They really feel incomplete and therefore to complete them or save them, they look for their mate. In a romantic setting, they lose their individuality. They could be defined as clinging in an attempt to get their partner closer, but in most cases, it just makes them more distant. Adults who are anxiously attached are often seeking approval for their anxieties.

Avoidant Attachment Styles

This is the kind that literally goes crazy the moment things get a little serious. Individuals who have avoidant attachment styles as adults sometimes pull away from romantic relationships. When they fear that a relationship is getting too serious, they push their partners away. They think they wouldn't gain anything from having a partner because they are so independent; in fact, they may feel stifled by intimacy and dependency. Adults who are in an avoidant relationship are more likely to choose short-term, casual relationships over committed ones. They equate relationships with loss of independence. For them relationships are a big burden causing them suffocation.

Disorganized Attachment Styles

Adults with disorganized attachment styles yearn for emotional closeness and affection yet are afraid of being overly reliant on romantic relationships. They can be erratic in their mood swings and overtaken by their emotions in relationships. As a result, individuals frequently find themselves in turbulent and uncertain relationships. When they feel insecure emotionally, they cling to their partners, but when things become too personal, they push them away. They are the right mix of anxious and avoidant types.

The types of parents one had while growing up affects our romantic relationships later in our lives. Let's delve a little deeper into it.

Early experiences with caregivers significantly shape adult relationship patterns. Individuals who endured emotionally abusive, highly critical or rejecting parenting often grapple with relationship anxiety, abandonment fears and difficulties with emotional vulnerability and trust in adulthood. Research by Hyun (2019) highlights these long-lasting effects of childhood experiences on adult relationships. Similarly, Kim et al. (2021) found that harsh parenting correlates with the development of anxious, avoidant or disorganisedattachment styles in adulthood. These attachment patterns can lead to confusion in interpersonal dynamics, making it challenging for individuals to navigate the delicate balance between seeking closeness and maintaining emotional distance in their relationships.

Parenting Styles -Baumrind (1971) explained patterns of parental authority.

The research by Cho et al. (2022) explores how different parenting styles influence young adults' behaviour in romantic relationships. Emerging adults raised by authoritarian mothers (those who are strict and demand obedience) tend to show higher levels of commitment in their romantic relationships. This might be because they're accustomed to rigid structures and clear expectations.On the other hand, those raised by authoritative mothers (who are firm but also warm and responsive) are more likely to compromise in their relationships. This could be because they've learned to balance their needs with others through open communication.

Interestingly, when it comes to the young adults' own approach to relationships, those who adopt an authoritative style themselves tend to be more willing to compromise but show less commitment to their romantic partners. This suggests they value flexibility and mutual understanding, but might be less inclined to commit fully. The study found no significant link between an authoritarian approach in relationships and either compromise or commitment levels.

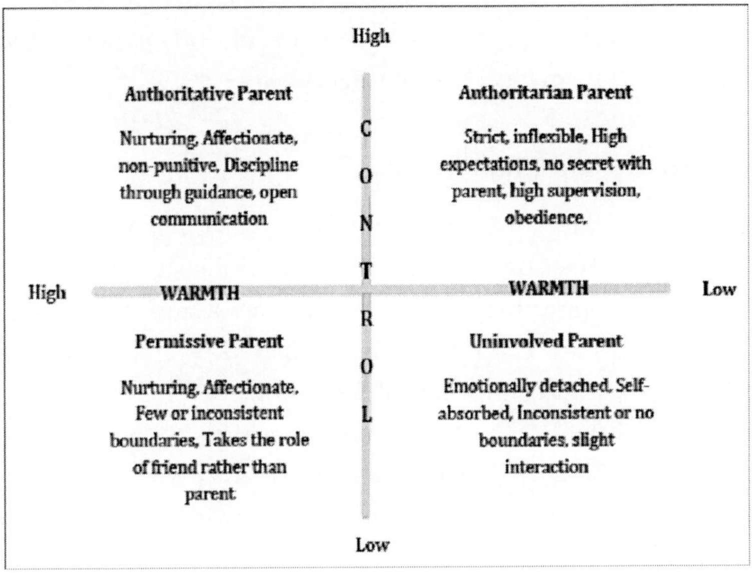

A compelling study by Fathi et al. (2011) explored the intricate connections between parenting styles, attachment patterns and marital infidelity. The research findings revealed a notable correlation between specific attachment styles and the propensity for extramarital affairs. Individuals who engaged in infidelity within their marriages predominantly exhibited an avoidant attachment style, characterised by emotional distance and discomfort with intimacy. Furthermore, the study uncovered a significant positive relationship between authoritarian parenting styles and the development of avoidant attachment patterns in children. This suggests that rigid, controlling parental behaviours may contribute to the formation of attachment styles that potentially increase vulnerability to marital infidelity later in life. These insights underscore the profound influence of early familial dynamics on adult relationship behaviours, offering valuable perspectives on the complex interplay between childhood experiences, attachment formation and marital fidelity.

Chemistry and Pheromones

Chemistry and pheromones play a significant role in romantic attraction, operating at a biological level that influences our subconscious preferences and responses. Pheromones are chemical signals released by the body that can trigger social and sexual behaviours in others, subtly affecting how we perceive and are drawn to potential partners. These chemical cues can enhance the feeling of "chemistry," that inexplicable sense of connection and attraction between individuals.

Additionally, hormones such as dopamine, oxytocin and serotonin are involved in the processes of attraction and bonding, contributing to the emotional highs and feelings of attachment we experience in romantic relationships. This biological interplay ensures that attraction is not solely based on physical appearance or shared interests but also on an innate chemical compatibility that enhances the depth and intensity of our connections.

Matching Hypothesis

According to the psychological concept known as the "matching hypothesis," people are likelier to start and sustain romantic relationships with people who share their physical appearance and other desirable characteristics. According to this theory, people look for mates who are nearly comparable in terms of desirability because they think that matching on these dimensions can result in more fulfilling and stable relationships. According to the matching hypothesis, people choose mates who they believe are on the same level as them by evaluating their own worth. This lowers the possibility of rejection and raises the possibility of mutual attraction and compatibility.

The principle of homophily, the tendency of individuals to associate and bond with others, who are similar to them, can be applied to explain such similarities (Jia et al., 2015).

Complementarity Hypothesis

The dynamics of romantic attraction encompass two contrasting yet equally intriguing phenomena: aspirational positive assortative mating and the complementarity hypothesis. While the former suggests that individuals seek partners who mirror their own qualities to some degree, the latter—often encapsulated in the popular adage "opposites attract"—proposes a different pathway to romantic harmony. The complementarity hypothesis posits that individuals are drawn to partners whose attributes differ from, yet complement, their own attributes. This theory suggests that romantic relationships thrive when partners possess distinct characteristics that balance and enhance one another, creating a harmonious whole. For example, an extroverted individual might find themselves attracted to an introvert, withtheir contrasting social tendencies fostering a balanced dynamic. By embracing and leveraging these differences, couples can potentially achieve a more robust and fulfilling partnership, where each individual's strengths compensate for the other's limitations, ultimately leading to a more rounded and satisfying relationship experience (Dryer & Horowitz, 1997).

Subconscious Modelling

When people look for romantic connections, subconscious modelling plays an important role. This idea relates to the unconsciously developed patterns and behaviours that result from our early experiences, especially those that we saw in our primary caregivers and other significant individuals when we were young. Our expectations, tastes and reactions in romantic situations are influenced by these early models. People, who were raised in a home where love and communication were freely shared, may unconsciously look for companions who behave in a similar way. On the other hand, early relationship experiences with conflict or emotional distance can result in subconscious avoidance or attachment problems in later romantic relationships. Not only can subconscious modelling affect the kinds of partners we are drawn to, but it also affects how we handle intimacy, resolve problems and show love. It can be quite helpful to recognize these unconscious effects in order to stop toxic patterns and create happier, more satisfying romantic relationships.

Personality

In the realm of romantic attraction, certain personal qualities stand out as universally appealing, fostering deep emotional connections and positive interactions between partners. Empathy, kindness and a well-developed sense of humor are highly valued traits, as they contribute to the creation of a supportive, enjoyable and nurturing relationship dynamic. These qualities form the bedrock of mutual understanding and respect, facilitating effective communication and emotional support, particularly during challenging times.

A good sense of humor, in particular, serves as a powerful tool for enhancing daily interactions and alleviating stress, thereby strengthening the bond between partners. Confidence is another attractive attribute, often perceived as a sign of security and reliability, suggesting a partner capable of navigating life's challenges with assurance.

Moreover, qualities such as intelligence and ambition are frequently sought after, as they indicate a partner who is not only capable but also motivated to contribute positively to the relationship's growth and stability. These traits suggest a potential for personal development and shared progress which can be incredibly attractive in a long-term partnership.

Ultimately, the most appealing individuals are those who can forge genuine emotional connections, making their partners feel valued, understood and uplifted. High levels of Conscientiousness, Extraversion, and Agreeableness are generally desirable, while people tend to prefer partners with lower levels of Neuroticism than themselves. This preference suggests a desire for emotional stability and positive interactions in relationships.

Interestingly, the criteria for attractiveness shift depending on the nature of the relationship sought. For short-term sexual partnerships, both men and women prioritize physical attributes such as attractiveness, health, sex drive and athleticism. In contrast, when considering long-term romantic relationships, the focus shifts towards similarity and socially appealing personality traits, including intelligence, honesty and warmth (Markey & Markey, 2007).

However, it's crucial to recognise that attraction is a highly individualised phenomenon. What one person finds appealing may differ significantly from another's preferences. Moreover, perceptions of attractiveness are not formed in a vacuum but are heavily influenced by sociological and cultural factors. The complexity of romantic attraction stems from the interplay of various psychological elements, personal experiences and individual values.

This multifaceted nature of attraction underscores the diversity of human relationships and the unique dynamics that shape each romantic connection. It reminds us that while general trends exist, the path to finding a compatible partner is often as unique as the individuals involved.

References

Abdi, M. R., Nazari, A. M., &Zabihzadeh, A. (2012). Internet infidelity: Exploration of attitudes towards partners' internetbehaviours. *Zahedan Journal of Research in Medical Sciences*, *14*(9).

Abell, L., & Brewer, G.(2016).Machiavellianism, perceived quality of alternative mates, and resistance to mate guarding. *Personality and Individual Differences*, *101*, 236-239.

Alavi,M., Mei, T.K., &Mehdinezhad, S.A. (2018). The Dark Triad of personality and infidelity intentions: The moderating role of relationship experience. *Personality and Individual Differences*, *128*, 49-54.

Alavi, M.,Mei, T.K., &Mehdinezhad, S.A. (2018). The Dark Triad of personality and infidelity intentions: The moderating role of relationship experience. *Personality and Individual Differences*, *128*, 49-54.

Albury, K., &Crawford, K.(2012). Sexting, consent and young people's ethics: Beyond Megan's Story. *Continuum*, *26*(3), 463-473.

Ali,F.,& Chamorro-Premuzic, T.(2010). The dark side of love and life satisfaction: Associations with intimate relationships, psychopathy and Machiavellianism. *Personality and individual differences*, *48*(2), 228-233.

Allen, E.S., Atkins, D.C. (2005). The multidimensional and developmental nature of infidelity: Practical applications. *Journal of clinical psychology*, *61*(11), 1371-1382.

Allen, E.S., Atkins, D.C.(2012). The association of divorce and extramarital sex in a representative US sample. *Journal of Family Issues,* 33(11), 1477-1493.

Allen, E.S., Rhoades, G.K., Stanley, S.M., Markman, H.J., Williams, T., Melton, J., & Clements, M.L. (2008). Premarital precursors of marital infidelity. *Family process, 47*(2), 243-259.

Allen, E.S., Rhoades, G.K., Stanley, S.M., Markman, H. J., Williams, T., Melton, J., & Clements, M.L. (2008).Premarital precursors of marital infidelity. *Family process*, *47*(2), 243-259.

Anderson, W., & DiTunnariello, N. (2016).Aggressive humor as a negative relational maintenance behaviour during times of conflict. *The Qualitative Report*, *21*(8), 1513-1530.

Andrade, A., Wachelke, J., & Howat-Rodrigues, A.B.C.(2015). Relationship satisfaction in young adults: Gender and love dimensions. *Interpersona: An International Journal on Personal Relationships*, *9*(1), 19-31.

Andrew, J., Cooke, M., &Muncer, S.J. (2008). The relationship between empathy and Machiavellianism: An alternative to empathizing–systemizing theory. *Personality and Individual Differences*, *44*(5), 1203-1211.

Andrew, J., Cooke, M., &Muncer, S. J. (2008). The relationship between empathy and Machiavellianism: An alternative to empathizing–systemizing theory. *Personality and Individual Differences*, *44*(5), 1203-1211.

Anqi, X.U.(2016).The establishment and dissolution of marriage. *The Chinese Family Today*, 129.

Apostolou, M.(2022). Catch me if you can: Strategies for hiding infidelity. *Personality and Individual Differences*, *189*, 111494.

Apostolou, M., &Tekeş, B.(2023).Fear of Relationship Commitment and Singlehood. *Evolutionary Psychological Science*, 1-9.

Arantes, J., Barros, F., & Oliveira, H. M. (2020). Extradyadic behaviours and gender: How do they relate with sexual desire, relationship quality, and attractiveness. *Frontiers in psychology*, *10*, 481350.

Arikewuyo, A.O., Eluwole, K.K., & Özad, B. (2021). Influence of lack of trust on romantic relationship problems: The mediating role of partner cell phone snooping. *Psychological Reports*, *124*(1), 348-365.

Arnocky, S., Albert, G., Carré, J.M., & Ortiz, T.L. (2018). Intrasexual competition mediates the relationship between men's testosterone and mate retention behaviour. *Physiology &Behaviour*, *186*, 73-78.

Aron, A., & Aron, E. N. (1997).Self-expansion motivation and including others in the self.

Atari, M., Barbaro,N., Sela, Y., Shackelford, T.K., & Chegeni, R.(2017). The Big Five personality dimensions and mate retention behaviours in Iran. *Personality and Individual Differences*, *104*, 286-290.

Atkins, D.C., Baucom, D.H., & Jacobson, N.S.(2001). Understanding infidelity: correlates in a national random sample. *Journal of family psychology*, *15*(4), 735.

Attridge, M.(2013). Jealousy and relationship closeness: Exploring the good (reactive) and bad (suspicious) sides of romantic jealousy. *SAGE open*, *3*(1), 2158244013476054.

Ayres, J.(1983). Strategies to maintain relationships: Their identification and perceived usage. *Communication Quarterly*, *31*(1), 62-67.

Backstrom, L., Armstrong, E. A., & Puentes, J. (2012).Women's negotiation of cunnilingus in college hookups and relationships. *Journal of Sex Research*, *49*(1), 1-12.

Baldwin, M.W., Fehr, B., Keedian, E., Seidel, M., & Thomson, D.W. (1993). An exploration of the relational schemata underlying attachment styles: Self-report and lexical decision approaches. *Personality and social psychology bulletin*, *19*(6), 746-754.

Barbaro, N., Pham, M. N., Shackelford, T. K., & Zeigler-Hill, V. I. R. G. I. L. (2016).Insecure romantic attachment dimensions and frequency of mate retention behaviours. *Personal Relationships*, *23*(3), 605-618.

Barrense-Dias, Y., Berchtold, A., Surís, J.C., & Akre, C. (2017). Sexting and the definition issue. *Journal of adolescent health*, *61*(5), 544-554.

Barta, W.D., & Kiene, S.M(2005). Motivations for infidelity in heterosexual dating couples: The roles of.

Barta, W. D., & Kiene, S. M.(2005). Motivations for infidelity in heterosexual dating couples: The roles of gender, personality differences, and sociosexual orientation. *Journal of Social and Personal Relationships*, *22*(3), 339-360.

Bataller, S.A.(2002). Tratamiento conductual de un trastorno de celos patológicos. *Cuadernos de medicina psicosomática y psiquiatría de enlace*, (62), 83-96.

Baumeister, R.F., Wotman, S. R., & Stillwell, A. M. (1993). Unrequited love: On heartbreak, anger, guilt, spiritlessness, and humiliation. *Journal of personality and social psychology*, *64*(3), 377.

Baumgartner, S.E., Sumter, S.R., Peter,J., & Valkenburg, P.M. (2015). Sexual self-presentation on social network sites: Who does it and how is it perceived?. *Computers in Human Behaviour*, *50*, 91-100.

Baumrind, D. (1971). Current patterns of parental authority. *Developmental Psychology, 4*, 1–103.

Beaulieu-Pelletier,G., Philippe, F.L., Lecours, S., & Couture, S. (2011).The role of attachment avoidance in extradyadic sex. *Attachment & Human Development*, *13*(3), 293-313.

Beckmeyer, J.J.(2023).Sexting and the Dynamics of Emerging Adults' Romantic Partnerships. *Sexuality & Culture*, 1-17.

Beltrán-Morillas, A.M., Valor-Segura, I., & Expósito, F.(2019). Unforgiveness motivations in romantic relationships experiencing infidelity: Negative affect and anxious attachment to the partner as predictors. *Frontiers in psychology*, *10*, 437353.

Benotsch, E.G., Snipes, D.J., Martin, A.M., & Bull, S.S. (2013).Sexting, substance use, and sexual risk behaviour in young adults. *Journal of adolescent health*, *52*(3), 307-313.

BEN-ZE'EV, A. (2004). Love Online: Emotions on the Internet.[Electronic version].

Biolcati, R., Pupi, V., & Mancini, G. (2022). Cyber dating abuse and ghosting behaviours: personality and gender roles in romantic relationships. *Current issues in personality psychology*, *10*(3), 240.

Birnbaum, G.E., & Reis, H.T. (2019).Evolved to be connected: The dynamics of attachment and sex over the course of romantic relationships. *Current opinion in psychology*, *25*, 11-15.

Blow, A.J., & Hartnett, K.(2005).Infidelity in committed relationships-A substantive review. *Journal of marital and family therapy*, *31*(2), 217-233.

Blumenstock, S.M.(2024).Romantic attachment and sexual desire: The role of desire target. *The Journal of Sex Research*, *61*(2), 313-323.

Boddy, C.R. (2011).Corporate psychopaths, bullying and unfair supervision in the workplace. *Journal of business ethics*, *100*(3), 367-379.

Bonfá-Araujo, B., Lima-Costa, A. R., Hauck-Filho, N., & Jonason, P. K. (2022).Considering sadism in the shadow of the Dark Triad traits: A meta-analytic review of the Dark Tetrad. *Personality and Individual Differences*, *197*, 111767.

Borgogna, N.C., Meyer, C.L., Trussell, M.R., Garos, S.,& Kraus, S. W. (2023).Further understanding the correlations between sexting and mental health: considerations for sex and sexual identity. *Cyberpsychology, Behaviour, and Social Networking*, *26*(5), 323-331.

Bowlby,J.(1979).The bowlby-ainsworth attachment theory. *Behavioural and Brain Sciences*, *2*(4), 637-638.

Braithwaite, S.R., Delevi, R., & Fincham, F.D.(2010). Romantic relationships and the physical and mental health of college students. *Personal relationships*, *17*(1), 1-12.

Braithwaite, S.,& Holt-Lunstad, J. (2017).Romantic relationships and mental health. *Current Opinion in Psychology*, *13*, 120-125.

Brand, R.J., Markey, C. M., Mills, A., & Hodges, S. D. (2007).Sex differences in self-reported infidelity and its correlates. *Sex roles*, *57*, 101-109.

Brem, M.J., Spiller, L.C., & Vandehey, M.A. (2015). Online mate-retention tactics on Facebook are associated with relationship aggression. *Journal of interpersonal violence, 30*(16), 2831-2850.

Brennan, K.A., & Shaver, P.R.(1995). Dimensions of adult attachment, affect regulation, and romantic relationship functioning. *Personality and social psychology bulletin, 21*(3), 267-283.

Brewer, G., & Abell, L. (2015).Machiavellianism and sexual behaviour: Motivations, deception and infidelity. *Personality and Individual Differences, 74*, 186-191.

Brewer, G., & Abell, L.(2015). Machiavellianism in long-term relationships: Competition, mate retention and sexual coercion. *Scandinavian Journal of Psychology, 56*(3), 357-362.

Brewer, G., Bennett, C., Davidson, L., Ireen, A., Phipps, A. J., Stewart-Wilkes, D., & Wilson, B. (2018). Dark triad traits and romantic relationship attachment, accommodation, and control. *Personality and Individual Differences, 120*, 202-208.

Brewer, G., Parkinson, M., Pickles, A., Anson, J., & Mulinder, G. (2023).Dark Triad traits and relationship dissolution. *Personality and Individual Differences, 204*, 112045.

Bringle, R.G., Winnick, T., & Rydell, R. J. (2013).The prevalence and nature of unrequited love. *Sage Open, 3*(2), 2158244013492160.

Brotto, L.A., Woo, J.S., & Gorzalka, B.B.(2012).Differences in sexual guilt and desire in East Asian and Euro-Canadian men. *Journal of Sex Research, 49*(6), 594-602.

Bryant, C.M., Conger, R.D., Vangelisti, A.L., Reiss, H.T., & Fitzpatrick, M.A. (2002). Stability and change in relationships.

Bryant, F.B., & Veroff, J. (2017). *Savouring: A new model of positive experience*. Psychology Press.

Burgoon, J.K., Buller, D.B.,White, C.H., Afifi, W., & Buslig, A.L. (1999).The role of conversational involvement in deceptive interpersonal interactions. *Personality and Social Psychology Bulletin*, *25*(6), 669-686.

Burke, T.J., & Young, V.J. (2012).Sexual transformations and intimate behaviours in romantic relationships. *Journal of Sex Research*, *49*(5), 454-463.

Burkett, M.(2015). Sex (t) talk: A qualitative analysis of young adults' negotiations of the pleasures and perils of sexting. *Sexuality & culture*, *19*, 835-863.

Buss, D.M.(2018). Sexual and emotional infidelity: Evolved gender differences in jealousy prove robust and replicable. *Perspectives on psychological science*, *13*(2), 155-160.

Buss, D.M.(2019).The evolution of love in humans. *The new psychology of love*, *1*, 42-63.

Buss, D.M. i Schmitt, DP (1993). Sexual strategies theory: an evolutionary perspective on human mating. *Psychological review*, *100*(2), 204.

Buss, D.M., Shackelford, T.K. (1997). From vigilance to violence: mate retention tactics in married couples. *Journal of personality and social psychology*, *72*(2), 346.

Buss, D.M., Shackelford, T.K., & McKibbin, W.F. (2008).The mate retention inventory-short form (MRI-SF). *Personality and Individual Differences*, *44*(1), 322-334.

Buunk, A.P., Dijkstra,P., & Massar, K. (2018).The universal threat and temptation of extradyadic affairs. In *The Cambridge handbook of personal relationships* (pp. 353-364).Cambridge University Press.

Buunk, B.P., & Dijkstra, P. (2006).The ultimate betrayal? Infidelity and solidarity in close relationships.

In *Solidarity and prosocial behaviour: An integration of sociological and psychological perspectives* (pp. 111-124). Boston, MA: Springer US.

Campbell, W.K.(1999).Narcissism and romantic attraction. *Journal of Personality and social Psychology*, *77*(6), 1254.

Campbell, W.K., Foster, C.A., & Finkel, E. J. (2002). Does self-love lead to love for others? A story of narcissistic game playing. *Journal of personality and social psychology*, *83*(2), 340.

Campbell, W.K., Rudich, E.A., & Sedikides, C.(2002). Narcissism, self-esteem, and the positivity of self-view: Two portraits of self-love. *Personality and Social Psychology Bulletin*, *28*(3), 358-368.

Carroll, J. S., Padilla-Walker, L. M., Nelson, L. J., Olson, C. D., McNamara Barry, C., & Madsen, S. D. (2008). Generation XXX: Pornography acceptance and use among emerging adults. *Journal of adolescent research*, *23*(1), 6-30.

Carswell, K.L., & Impett, E.A.(2021). What fuels passion? An integrative review of competing theories of romantic passion. *Social and Personality Psychology Compass*, *15*(8), e12629.

Carver, K.,Joyner, K., & Udry, J. R. (2003).National estimates of adolescent romantic relationships. In *Adolescent romantic relations and sexual behaviour*,37-70.

Charny, I.W., & Parnass, S.(1995).The impact of extramarital relationships on the continuation of marriages. *Journal of Sex & Marital Therapy*, *21*(2), 100-115.

Cho, P.L.Y., Ong, A. S. E., & Cheung, H. S. (2022). Where authoritarianism is not always bad: Parenting styles and romantic relationship quality among emerging adults in Singapore. *Current Psychology*, 1-10.

Christian, E., Sellbom, M., & Wilkinson, R.B.(2017). Clarifying the associations between individual differences in general attachment styles and psychopathy. *Personality Disorders: Theory, Research, and Treatment*, *8*(4), 329.

Cole, T.(2001). Lying to the one you love: The use of deception in romantic relationships. *Journal of Social and Personal Relationships*, *18*(1), 107-129.

Collins, N.L., & Feeney, B.C.(2000). A safe haven: an attachment theory perspective on support seeking and caregiving in intimate relationships. *Journal of personality and social psychology*, *78*(6), 1053.

Collins, N.L., & Read, S. J. (1990).Adult attachment, working models, and relationship quality in dating couples. *Journal of personality and social psychology*, *58*(4), 644.

Collins, T.J., & Gillath, O.(2012). Attachment, breakup strategies, and associated outcomes: The effects of security enhancement on the selection of breakup strategies. *Journal of Research in Personality*, *46*(2), 210-222.

Collins, T.J., & Gillath, O.(2012). Attachment, breakup strategies, and associated outcomes: The effects of security enhancement on the selection of breakup strategies. *Journal of Research in Personality*, *46*(2), 210-222.

Collins, T.J., Thomas, A.F., & Harris, E. (2023). Unwanted and unfollowed: Defining ghosting and the role of social media unfollowing. *Personal Relationships*, *30*(3), 939-959.

Collins, W.A.(2003). More than myth: The developmental significance of romantic relationships during adolescence. *Journal of research on adolescence*, *13*(1), 1-24.

Conlon, K.E. (2019). Mate retention strategies of dominance-oriented and prestige-oriented romantic partners. *Evolutionary Psychological Science*, *5*, 317-327.

Currin, J.M., Evans, A.E., & Garos, S. (2023). In a relationship, who tends to sext first?. *Sexual and Relationship Therapy*, *38*(4), 586-602.

Curtis, J.M., &Susman, V. M. (1994). Factors related to fear of marriage. *Psychological reports*, *74*(3), 859-863.

Dainton, M.,& Aylor, B. (2002). Patterns of communication channel use in the maintenance of long-distance relationships. *Communication Research Reports*, *19*(2), 118-129.

Dainton, M., & Berkoski, L.(2013). Positive and negative maintenance behaviours, jealousy, and Facebook: Impacts on college students' romantic relationships. *Pennsylvania Communication Annual*, *69*(1), 35-50.

Dainton, M., & Gross, J.(2008).The use of negative behaviours to maintain relationships. *Communication Research Reports*, *25*(3), 179-191.

Dainton, M., & Stokes, A.(2015). College students' romantic relationships on Facebook: Linking the gratification for maintenance to Facebook maintenance activity and the experience of jealousy. *Communication Quarterly*, *63*(4), 365-383.

Danel, D. P., Siennicka, A., Glińska, K., Fedurek, P., Nowak-Szczepańska, N., Jankowska, E. A., & Lewandowski, Z. (2017).Female perception of a partner's mate value discrepancy and controlling behaviour in romantic relationships. *Acta Ethologica*, *20*, 1-8.

Daraj, L. R., Buhejji, M. R., Perlmutter, G., Jahrami, H., & Seeman, M. V. (2023). Ghosting: Abandonment in the Digital Era. *Encyclopedia*, *4*(1), 36-45

Davis, K.E., Kirkpatrick, L.A., & Levy, M.B. (2013).Stalking the Elusive Love Style: Attachment Styles, Love Styles. *Theoretical frameworks for personal relationships*, 179.

De Jong, D. C., & Reis, H. T. (2015). We do it best: Commitment and positive construals of sex. *Journal of Social and Clinical Psychology*, *34*(3), 181-202.

DePaulo, B. (2014). A singles studies perspective on mount marriage. *Psychological Inquiry*, *25*(1), 64-68.

DePaulo, B.M., & Morris,W.L. (2006).The unrecognized stereotyping and discrimination against singles. *Current Directions in Psychological Science*, *15*(5), 251-254.

DeWall, C.N., Lambert, N.M., Slotter, E. B., Pond Jr, R. S., Deckman, T., Finkel, E. J., & Fincham, F. D. (2011).So far away from one's partner, yet so close to romantic alternatives: avoidant attachment, interest in alternatives, and infidelity. *Journal of personality and social psychology*, *101*(6), 1302.

DeWall, C.N., Lambert, N.M., Slotter, EB., Pond Jr, R.S., Deckman, T., Finkel, E. J.,& Fincham, F.D. (2011).So far away from one's partner, yet so close to romantic alternatives: avoidant attachment, interest in alternatives, and infidelity. *Journal of personality and social psychology*, *101*(6), 1302.

Dindia, K., & Baxter, L.A.(1987).Strategies for maintaining and repairing marital relationships. *Journal of social and personal relationships*, *4*(2), 143-158.

Downey, G., & Feldman, S.I.(1996).Implications of rejection sensitivity for intimate relationships. *Journal of personality and social psychology*, *70*(6), 1327.

Downey, G., Bonica, C., & Rincon, C. (1999).Rejection sensitivity and adolescent romantic relationships. *The development of romantic relationships in adolescence*, 148-174.

Doyle, C., Douglas, E., & O'Reilly, G.(2021). The outcomes of sexting for children and adolescents: A systematic review of the literature. *Journal of adolescence*, *92*, 86-113.

Drouin, M., Coupe, M., & Temple, J. R. (2017). Is sexting good for your relationship? It depends.*Computers in Human Behaviour*, *75*, 749-756.

Dryer, D.C., & Horowitz, L.M. (1997). When do opposites attract? Interpersonal complementarity versus similarity. *Journal of personality and social psychology*, *72*(3), 592.

Dyrenforth, P.S., Kashy, D.A., Donnellan, M.B., & Lucas, R. E. (2010).Predicting relationship and life satisfaction from personality in nationally representative samples from three countries: the relative importance of actor, partner, and similarity effects. *Journal of personality and social psychology*, *99*(4), 690.

Eden, J. (2010). *"Nothing takes the taste out of peanut butter quite like unrequited love": Examining the effects of unrequited love relationships*. Arizona State University.

Ellis, N.K., &Ledbetter, A. M. (2015). Why might distance make the heart grow fonder?: A relational turbulence model investigation of the maintenance of long distance and geographically close romantic relationships. *Communication Quarterly*, *63*(5), 568-585.

Emmons, R.A. (1987). Narcissism: theory and measurement. *Journal of personality and social psychology*, *52*(1), 11.

Fathi, E., Gorji, Z., &Esmaeily, M. (2011).The Relationship between parenting styles and Attachment Styles in men and women with infidelity. *Procedia-Social and Behavioural Sciences*, *15*, 3743-3747.

Fehr, B.(2013).The social psychology of love. *The Oxford handbook of closerelationships*, 201-233.

Field, T.(2011). Romantic breakups, heartbreak and bereavement—Romantic breakups. *Psychology*,*2*(04), 382.

Field, T.(2017). Romantic breakup distress, betrayal and heartbreak: A review. *International Journal of Behavioural Research & Psychology*, *5*(2), 217-225.

Figueredo, A.J., Sefcek, J.A., &Jones, D.N.(2006). The ideal romantic partner personality. *Personality and Individual Differences*, *41*(3), 431-441.

Fincham, F.D., & Beach, S.R.(2014). I say a little prayer for you: Praying for partner increases commitment in romantic relationships. *Journal of Family Psychology*, *28*(5), 587.

Fincham, F.D., & May, R.W. (2017).Infidelity in romantic relationships. *Current opinion in psychology*, *13*, 70-74.

Firmin,M., Firmin, R., & Lorenzen, K. (2014).A qualitative analysis of loneliness dynamics involved with college long-distance relationships. *College Student Journal*, *48*(1), 57-71.

Fisher, A.N., & Sakaluk, J.K. (2020). Are single people a stigmatized 'group'? Evidence from examinations of social identity, entitativity, and perceived responsibility.*Journal of Experimental Social Psychology*, *86*, 103844.

Fletcher, G. J., Simpson, J.A., Campbell, L., & Overall, N.C.(2019).*The science of intimate relationships*. John Wiley & Sons.

Fletcher, G.J., Simpson, J.A., Campbell, L.,& Overall, N. C.(2015). Pair-bonding, romantic love and evolution: The curious case of Homo sapiens. *Perspectives on psychological science*, *10*(1), 20-36.

Floyd, K. (2016). Affection deprivation is associated with physical pain and poor sleep quality. *Communication Studies*, *67*(4), 379-398.

Forrai, M., Koban, K., & Matthes, J. (2023).Short-sighted ghosts. Psychological antecedents and consequences of ghosting others within emerging adults' romantic relationships and friendships. *Telematics and Informatics*, *80*, 101969.

Fox, B., & DeLisi, M.(2019). Psychopathic killers: A meta-analytic review of the psychopathy-homicide nexus. *Aggression and Violent Behaviour*, *44*, 67-79.

Franiuk, R., Cohen, D., & Pomerantz, E. M. (2002). Implicit theories of relationships: Implications for relationship satisfaction and longevity. *Personal Relationships*, *9*(4), 345-367.

Freedman, G., Powell, D. N., Le, B., & Williams, K. D. (2019). Ghosting and destiny: Implicit theories of relationships predict beliefs about ghosting. *Journal of Social and Personal Relationships*, *36*(3), 905-924.

Freud, S. (1905). Three essays on the theory of sexuality. *Se*, *7*, 125-243.

Frisco, M. L., Wenger, M.R., & Kreager, D. A. (2017). Extradyadic sex and union dissolution among young adults in opposite-sex married and cohabiting unions. *Social Science Research*, *62*, 291-304.

Furman, W.,& Simon, V.A. (2008). Homophily in adolescent romantic relationships. *Understanding peer influence in children and adolescents*, 203-224.

Gabriel, M.T., Critelli, J.W., & Ee, J.S. (1994).Narcissistic illusions in self-evaluations of intelligence and attractiveness. *Journal of personality*, *62*(1), 143-155.

Garbinsky, E.N., Gladstone, J. J., Nikolova, H., & Olson, J.

G. (2020). Love, lies, and money: Financial infidelity in romantic relationships. *Journal of Consumer Research*, *47*(1), 1-24.

Garofalo, C., Neumann, C. S., &Velotti, P. (2018). Difficulties in emotion regulation and psychopathic traits in violent offenders. *Journal of criminal justice*, *57*, 116-125.

Gewirtz-Meydan, A., Mitchell, K.J., & Rothman, E.F. (2018). What do kids think about sexting?. *Computers in Human Behaviour*, *86*, 256-265.

Ghiasi, N., Rasoal, D., Haseli, A., & Feli, R. (2024). The interplay of attachment styles and marital infidelity: A systematic review and meta-analysis. *Heliyon.*

Gibson, T. J. (2020). If You Want the Milk, Buy the Cow: A Study of Young Black Women's Experiences in Situationships.

Gill, A.D., & Stickle, T. R. (2016).Affective differences between psychopathy variants and genders in adjudicated youth. *Journal of abnormal child psychology*, *44*, 295-307.

Glass, S.P., & Wright, T.L.(1985).Sex differences in type of extramarital involvement and marital dissatisfaction. *Sex Roles*, *12*, 1101-1120.

Gómez-García, G., Romero-Rodríguez, J. M., Rodríguez-Jiménez, C., & Ramos Navas-Parejo, M. (2020). Sexting among university students: Links to internet addiction and psychological variables. *Publ. J. Drug Alcohol Res*, *9*, 1-16.

Gonzalez, C. C. (2011). Personal and perceived partner commitment and trust as predictors of relationship satisfaction in long-distance and proximally close dating relationships of graduate students.

Goodboy, A.K., & Bolkan, S. (2011).Attachment and the use of negative relational maintenance behaviours in romantic relationships. *Communication Research Reports*, *28*(4), 327-336.

Goodboy, A.K., Myers, S.A., Members of Investigating Communication. (2010). Relational quality indicators and love styles as predictors of negative relational maintenance behaviours in romantic relationships. *Communication Reports*, *23*(2), 65-78.

Gordon, A.M., Impett, E.A., Kogan, A., Oveis, C., & Keltner, D. (2012). To have and to hold: gratitude promotes relationship maintenance in intimate bonds. *Journal of personality and social psychology*, *103*(2), 257.

Gottman, J.M., & Gottman, J.M.(1999). The sound marital house: A theory of marriage. *The marriage clinic: A scientifically based marital therapy*, 87-110.

Graham-Kevan, N., & Archer, J. (2009). Control tactics and partner violence in heterosexual relationships. *Evolution and Human Behaviour*, *30*(6), 445-452.

Guerrero, L. K., & Andersen, P.A.(1996).Jealousy experience and expression in romantic relationships. *Handbook of communication and emotion*, 155-188.

Guerrero, L.K., Anderson, P. L., & Afifi, W. A. (2017). Conceptualizing relational communication: Definitions and principles. *Close encounters: Communication in relationships*, 1-24.

Guest, C.,& Denes, A.(2022). Too much too soon? Perceived appropriateness of sexting across stages of relationship development and attachment tendencies among emerging adults. *Computers in Human Behaviour*, *137*, 107429.

Gupta, A. (2023, May 21). *12 surprising benefits of extramarital affairs for your marriage.* Bonobology.com. https://www.bonobology.com/benefits-extramarital-affairs/

Ha, T., Otten, R., McGill, S., & Dishion, T. J. (2019). The family and peer origins of coercion within adult romantic relationships: A longitudinal multimethod study across relationships contexts. *Developmental psychology*, *55*(1), 207.

Hackathorn, J., & Harvey, R.(2011). Sexual double standards: Bias in perceptions of cyber-infidelity. *Sexuality & Culture*, *15*, 100-113

Hare, R.D. (2003). Hare psychopathy checklist-revised (PCL-R) Toronto: Multi-Health Systems. *Inc* Harris, R. (2009). *ACT with love: Stop struggling, reconcile differences, and strengthen your relationship with acceptance and commitment.* New Harbinger Publications.

Haseli, A., Shariati, M., Nazari, A. M., Keramat, A., & Emamian, M. H. (2019). Infidelity and its associated factors: A systematic review. *The journal of sexual medicine*, *16*(8), 1155-1169.

Hatfield, E., & Rapson, R.L. (2011).Equity theory in close relationships. *Handbook of theories of social psychology*, *2*, 200-217.

Hazan, C., & Shaver, P.R.(1990). Love and work: An attachment-theoretical perspective. *Journal of Personality and social Psychology*, *59*(2), 270.

Hendrick, C., & Hendrick, S.(1986).A theory and method of love. *Journal of personality and social psychology*, *50*(2), 392.

Hendrick, C., & Hendrick, S. S. (2006).Styles of romantic love. *The new psychology of love*, 149-170.

Hertlein, K.M., & Ancheta, K.(2014). Advantages and disadvantages of technology in relationships: Findings from an open-ended survey. *The Qualitative Report, 19*(11), 1-11.

Hirschberger, G., Srivastava, S., Marsh, P., Cowan, C. P., & Cowan, P. A. (2009). Attachment, marital satisfaction, and divorce during the first fifteen years of parenthood. *Personal Relationships*, *16*(3), 401-420.

Holden, C. J., Shackelford, T. K., Zeigler-Hill, V., Miner, E. J., Kaighobadi, F., Starratt, V. G.,& Buss, D. M. (2014). Husband's esteem predicts his mate retention tactics. *Evolutionary Psychology*, *12*(3), 147470491401200311.

Holtzman, N.S., & Strube, M.J.(2013). People with dark personalities tend to create a physically attractive veneer. *Social Psychological and Personality Science*, *4*(4), 461-467.

Horan, S.M., Guinn, T.D., & Banghart, S.(2015). Understanding relationships among the dark triad personality profile and romantic partners' conflict communication. *Communication Quarterly*, *63*(2), 156-170.

Hughes, S., & Samuels, H.(2021). Dark desires: The Dark Tetrad and relationship control. *Personality and Individual Differences*, *171*, 110548.

Humeny, C., Forth, A., & Logan, J. (2021). Psychopathic traits predict survivors' experiences of domestic abuse. *Personality and Individual Differences*, *171*, 110497.

Hurley, D. B., & Kwon, P. (2013). Savouring helps most when you have little: Interaction between savouring the moment and uplifts on positive affect and satisfaction with life. *Journal of Happiness Studies*, *14*, 1261-1271.

Hyun, S. J. (2019).Analysis of the structural relationships

between romantic relationship satisfaction, childhood emotional abuse, adult attachment anxiety, and rejection sensitivity of university students. Graduate School of Hanyang University. http://www.riss.kr/link?id=T15035586

Ináncsi, T., Láng, A., & Bereczkei, T. (2015).Machiavellianism and adult attachment in general interpersonal relationships and close relationships. *Europe's journal of psychology*, *11*(1), 139.

Ináncsi, T., Láng, sA., & Bereczkei, T. (2016). A darker shade of love: Machiavellianism and positive assortative mating based on romantic ideals. *Europe's journal of psychology*, *12*(1), 137.

Jan Conradi, H., Gerlsma, C., Duijn, M. V., & Jonge, P.D. (2006).Internal and external validity of the experiences in close relationships questionnaire in an American and two Dutch samples. *The European journal of psychiatry*, *20*(4), 258-269.

Jeanfreau, M., Noguchi, K., Mong, M. D., & Stadthagen, H. (2018).Financial infidelity in couple relationships. *Journal of financial therapy*, *9*(1), 2.

Jia, T., Spivey, R. F., Szymanski, B., & Korniss, G. (2015).An analysis of the matching hypothesis in networks. *PloS one*, *10*(6), e0129804.

Joel, S., MacDonald, G., & Shimotomai, A.(2011). Conflicting pressures on romantic relationship commitment for anxiously attached individuals. *Journal of personality*, *79*(1), 51-74.

Johnson, H. D., Kent, A., & Yale, E.(2012).Examination of identity and romantic relationship intimacy associations with well-being in emerging adulthood. *Identity*, *12*(4), 296-319.

Jonason, P.K., & Kavanagh, P.(2010). The dark side of love: Love styles and the Dark Triad. *Personality and Individual Differences*, *49*(6), 606-610.

Jonason, P.K., Kaźmierczak, I., Campos, A.C., & Davis, M. D. (2021).Leaving without a word: Ghosting and the dark triad traits. *Acta Psychologica*, 220,103425.

Jonason, P. K., Luevano, V. X., & Adams, H. M.(2012). How the Dark Triad traits predict relationship choices. *Personality and Individual Differences*, *53*(3), 180-184.

Jones, D.N., & Paulhus, D.L.(2011).The role of impulsivity in the Dark Triad of personality. *Personality and Individual Differences*, *51*(5), 679-682.

Jones, D.N., & Paulhus, D. L. (2014).Introducing the short dark triad (SD3) a brief measure of dark personality traits. *Assessment*, *21*(1), 28-41.

Kaestle, C.E., & Halpern, C.T.(2007). What's love got to do with it? Sexual behaviours of opposite-sex couples through emerging adulthood. *Perspectives on sexual and reproductive health*, *39*(3), 134-140.

Kaighobadi, F., Shackelford, T. K., & Goetz, A. T. (2009). From mate retention to murder: Evolutionary psychological perspectives on men's partner-directed violence. *Review of General Psychology*, *13*(4), 327-334.

Kaighobadi, F., Shackelford,T. K., & Weekes-Shackelford, V. A. (2012). Do women pretend to orgasm to retain a mate?. *Archives of Sexual Behaviour*, *41*, 1121-1125.

Kay, C., & Courtice, E.L. (2022).An empirical, accessible definition of "ghosting" as a relationship dissolution method. *Personal Relationships*, *29*(2), 386-411.

Kelmer, G., Rhoades, G.K., Stanley, S., & Markman, H. J. (2013).Relationship quality, commitment, and stability in long-distance relationships. *Family process*, *52*(2), 257-270.

Kerckhoff, A. C.,& Davis, K. E. (1962). Value consensus and need complementarity in mate selection. *American sociological review*, 295-303.

Khattar, V., Huete, N.,& Navarro, R.(2023). Attachment insecurity and breadcrumbing engagement in young adults: a cross-sectional, cross-country study in India and Spain. *BMC psychology*, *11*(1), 356.

Kim, S., Baek, M., & Park, S.(2021). Association of Parent–child Experiences with Insecure Attachment in Adulthood: A Systematic Review and Meta-analysis. Journal of Family Theory & Review, 13(1), 58–76.

King, M., Holt, V., & Nazareth, I.(2007). Women's views of their sexual difficulties: Agreement and disagreement with clinical diagnoses. *Archives of Sexual Behaviour*, *36*, 281-288.

Knee, C.R.(1998). Implicit theories of relationships: Assessment and prediction of romantic relationship initiation, coping, and longevity. *Journal of Personality and Social Psychology*, *74*(2), 360.

Kobak, R.R., & Sceery, A.(1988). Attachment in late adolescence: Working models, affect regulation, and representations of self and others. *Child development*, 135-146.

Koessler, R. B., Kohut, T., & Campbell, L.(2019).Integration and expansion of qualitative analyses of relationship dissolution through ghosting.

Krapf, S.(2018). Moving in or breaking up? The role of distance in the development of romantic relationships. *European Journal of Population*, *34*(3), 313-336.

Kyranides, M.N., Kokkinou, A., Imran, S., & Cetin, M. (2023). Adult attachment and psychopathic traits:

Investigating the role of gender, maternal and paternal factors. *Current Psychology*, *42*(6), 4672-4681.

Lad, B., & Mansukhani, S. (2023). A correlational study between dass scales and attachment styles in ghosted Indian adults. *Karnavati Journal of Multidisciplinary Studies*, *1*(2), 64-82.

Lamkin, J., Campbell, W.K., & Miller, J.D. (2015). An exploration of the correlates of grandiose and vulnerable narcissism in romantic relationships: Homophily, partner characteristics, and dyadic adjustment. *Personality and Individual Differences*, *79*, 166-171.

Langlais, M. R.,Surra, C. A., Anderson, E. R., & Priem, J. (2017).Differentiating declining commitment and breakup using commitment to wed. *Journal of family studies*, *23*(3), 352-370.

Langlais, M., Citrano, E., Rentería, L., Gica, R., & Ormsbee, M. (2024). Where Did You Go?The Psychological and Physiological Consequences of Ghosting in Romantic Relationships. *Sexuality & Culture*, 1-16.

Langlois, J. H., Kalakanis, L., Rubenstein, A. J., Larson, A., Hallam, M., & Smoot, M. (2000). Maxims or myths of beauty? A meta-analytic and theoretical review. *Psychological bulletin*, *126*(3), 390.

Laursen, B., & Williams, V. A. (1997).Perceptions of interdependence and closeness in family and peer relationships among adolescents with and without romantic partners. *New Directions for Child and Adolescent Development*, *1997*(78), 3-20.

Leach, L.S., Butterworth, P., Olesen, S. C., & Mackinnon, A. (2013).Relationship quality and levels of depression and anxiety in a large population-based survey. *Social psychiatry and psychiatric epidemiology*, *48*, 417-425.

Lebow, H. I. (n.d.). Unrequited love: Meaning, signs, and tips to overcome it. Retrieved from https://psychcentral.com/health/unrequited-love-meaning#what-is-unrequited-love

Lee, J. A. (1973). *Colours of love: An exploration of the ways of loving.* New Press.

Lee, J. Y., & Pistole, M.C.(2012).Predictors of satisfaction in geographically close and long-distance relationships. *Journal of Counseling Psychology*, *59*(2), 303.

LeFebvre, L. E.,& Fan, X. (2020). Ghosted? Navigating strategies for reducing uncertainty and implications surrounding ambiguous loss. *Personal Relationships*, *27*(2), 433-459.

Lewandowski, G., & Bizzoco, N.(2007). Addition through subtraction: Growth following the dissolution of a low quality relationship. *The Journal of Positive Psychology, 2(1),* 40-54.

Lindová J. Mate Retention. In: Shackelford TK, ed. *The Cambridge Handbook of Evolutionary Perspectives on Sexual Psychology.* Cambridge Handbooks in Psychology. Cambridge University Press; 2022:343-373.

Lindová, J., Klapilová, K., Johnson, D., Vobořilová, A., Chlápková, B., & Havlíček, J. (2019). Non-verbal mate retention behaviour in women and its relation to couple's relationship adjustment and satisfaction. *Ethology*, *125*(12), 925-939.

Liong, M., & Cheng, G. H. L.(2019). Objectifying or liberating? Investigation of the effects of sexting on body image. *The Journal of Sex Research*, *56*(3), 337-344.

Lippman, J. R., & Campbell, S. W. (2014).Damned if you do, damned if you don't… if you're a girl: Relational and normative contexts of adolescent sexting in the United States. *Journal of Children and Media*, *8*(4), 371-386.

Liu, C.(2000).A theory of marital sexual life. *Journal of Marriage and Family*, *62*(2), 363-374.

Lopes, G.S., & Shackelford, T. K. (2019).Disengaged, exhaustive, benevolent: Three distinct strategies of mate retention. *Journal of Social and Personal Relationships*, *36*(9), 2677-2692.

Macenczak L.A., Campbell, S., Henley, A.B., & Campbell, W. K. (2016).Direct and interactive effects of narcissism and power on overconfidence. *Personality and Individual Differences*, *91*, 113-122.

Maguire, K. C., & Kinney, T. A. (2010).When distance is problematic: Communication, coping, and relational satisfaction in female college students' long-distance dating relationships. *Journal of Applied Communication Research*, *38*(1), 27-46.

Marcum, C. D., Higgins, G. E., & Nicholson, J. (2017). I'm watching you: Cyberstalking behaviours of university students in romantic relationships. *American journal of criminal justice*, *42*, 373-388.

Mark, K. P., Janssen, E., & Milhausen, R. R. (2011). Infidelity in heterosexual couples: Demographic, interpersonal, and personality-related predictors of extradyadic sex. *Archives of sexual behaviour*, *40*, 971-982.

Mark, K. P., Janssen, E., & Milhausen, R. R.(2011). Infidelity in heterosexual couples: Demographic, interpersonal, and personality-related predictors of extradyadic sex. *Archives of sexual behaviour*, *40*, 971-982.

Markey, P. M.& Markey, C. N. (2007). Romantic ideals, romantic obtainment, and relationship experiences: The complementarity of interpersonal traits among romantic partners. *Journal of social and Personal Relationships*, *24*(4), 517-533.

Marques, D. Muslukhov, I., Guerreiro, T., Beznosov, K., & Carric¸o, L. (2016). Snooping on mobile phones: Prevalence and trends. Symposium on usable privacy and security (pp. 159–174). Denver, CO: USENIX Association

Marshall, T.C., Bejanyan, K., & Ferenczi, N. (2013). Attachment styles and personal growth following romantic breakups: The mediating roles of distress, rumination, and tendency to rebound. *PloS one*, *8*(9), e75161.

Mattingly, B.A. Clark, E. M., Weidler, D. J., Bullock, M., Hackathorn, J., & Blankmeyer, K. (2011). Sociosexual orientation, commitment, and infidelity: A mediation analysis. *The Journal of social psychology*, *151*(3), 222-226.

Mattingly, B. A., Wilson, K., Clark, E. M., Bequette, A. W., & Weidler, D. J. (2010). Foggy faithfulness: Relationship quality, religiosity, and the perceptions of dating infidelity scale in an adult sample. *Journal of Family Issues*, *31*(11), 1465-1480.

Maucione, K. (2023). Perceptions of Long Distance Relationships

McDaniel, B. T., & Drouin, M. (2015). Sexting among married couples: Who is doing it, and are they more satisfied?. *Cyberpsychology, Behaviour, and Social Networking*, *18*(11), 628-634.

McHoskey, J. W. (2001).Machiavellianism and personality dysfunction. *Personality and Individual Differences*, *31*(5), 791-798.

McKibbin, W. F., Miner, E. J., Shackelford, T. K., Ehrke, A. D., & Weekes-Shackelford, V. A. (2014). Men's mate retention varies with men's personality and their partner's personality. *Personality and individual differences*, *56*, 62-67.

McLeod, S.(2007).Maslow's hierarchy of needs. *Simply psychology*, *1*(1-18).

McNulty, J. K., Wenner, C. A., & Fisher, T. D. (2016). Longitudinal associations among relationship satisfaction, sexual satisfaction, and frequency of sex in early marriage. *Archives of sexual behaviour*, *45*, 85-97.

McQueen, P.(2021).Sexual interactions and sexual infidelity. *The Journal of Ethics*, *25*(4), 449-466.

Meier, A. & Allen, G.(2009). Romantic relationships from adolescence to young adulthood: Evidence from the National Longitudinal Study of Adolescent Health. *The Sociological Quarterly*, *50*(2), 308-335.

Meltzer, A. L. (2020). Women can benefit from sexual and physical valuation in the context of a romantic relationship. *Personality and Social Psychology Bulletin*, *46*(2), 243-257.

Meltzer, A. L., Makhanova, A., Hicks, L. L., French, J. E., McNulty, J. K., & Bradbury, T. N. (2017).Quantifying the sexual afterglow: The lingering benefits of sex and their implications for pair-bonded relationships. *Psychological Science*, *28*(5), 587-598.

Merolla, A. J. (2012).Connecting here and there: A model of long-distance relationship maintenance. *Personal Relationships*, *19*(4), 775-795.

Metts, S.(1989).An exploratory investigation of deception in close relationships. *Journal of Social and Personal relationships*, *6*(2), 159-179.

Miano, A(2017).Romantic relationship dysfunction in borderline personality disorder.

Mikulincer, M., & Nachshon, O. (1991).Attachment styles and patterns of self-disclosure. *Journal of personality and social psychology*, *61*(2), 321.

Miller, J. D., Hoffman, B. J., Gaughan, E. T., Gentile, B., Maples, J., & Keith Campbell, W. (2011). Grandiose and vulnerable narcissism: A nomological network analysis. *Journal of personality*, *79*(5), 1013-1042.

Miner, E. J., Shackelford, T. K., & Starratt, V. G. (2009). Mate value of romantic partners predicts men's partner-directed verbal insults. *Personality and Individual Differences*, *46*(2), 135-139.

Miner, E. J., Starratt, V. G.,& Shackelford, T. K. (2009). It's not all about her: Men's mate value and mate retention. *Personality and Individual Differences*, *47*(3), 214-218.

Mogilski, J. K.,& Welling, L. L. (2017). Staying friends with an ex: Sex and dark personality traits predict motivations for post-relationship friendship. *Personality and Individual Differences*, *115*, 114-119.

Montoya, R. M.& Horton, R. S. (2013).A meta-analytic investigation of the processes underlying the similarity-attraction effect. *Journal of Social and Personal Relationships*, *30*(1), 64-94.

Morelli, M., Bianchi, D., Baiocco, R., Pezzuti, L.,& Chirumbolo, A. (2016).Sexting, psychological distress and dating violence among adolescents and young adults. *Psicothema.*

Morrongiello, B. A.,Hou, S., & Cox, A. (2019).Keeping pre-adolescents safe: Parental knowledge and safety promotion strategies. *Journal of Applied Developmental Psychology*, *62*, 59-65.

Munsch, C. L. (2015). Her support, his support: Money, masculinity, and marital infidelity. *American Sociological Review*, *80*(3), 469-495.

Nascimento, B. S., & Little, A. (2020). Mate retention behaviours and jealousy in hypothetical mate-poaching situations: Measuring the effects of sex, context, and rivals' attributes. *Evolutionary Psychological Science*, *6*(1), 20-29.

Nascimento, B. S., & Little, A.(2020). Mate retention behaviours and jealousy in hypothetical mate-poaching situations: Measuring the effects of sex, context, and rivals' attributes. *Evolutionary Psychological Science*, *6*(1), 20-29.

Navarro, R., Larrañaga, E., Yubero, S., & Víllora, B. (2021). Individual, interpersonal and relationship factors associated with ghosting intention and behaviours in adult relationships: Examining the associations over and above being a recipient of ghosting. *Telematics and informatics*, *57*, 101513.

Neustaedter, C., & Greenberg, S. (2012, May).Intimacy in long-distance relationships over video chat. In *Proceedings of the SIGCHI conference on human factors in computing systems* (pp. 753-762).

Nicholson, Jodi. (2020).Positive Communication in Romantic Relationships.

Ogolsky, B. G., & Stafford, L.(2023). A systematic review of relationship maintenance: Reflecting back and looking to the future. *Personal Relationships*, *30*(1), 19-43.

Overall, N. C., & Sibley, C. G.(2008).Attachment and attraction toward romantic partners versus relevant alternatives within daily interactions. *Personality and Individual Differences*, *44*(5), 1126-1137.

Pancani, L., Mazzoni, D., Aureli, N., & Riva, P. (2021). Ghosting and orbiting: An analysis of victims' experiences. *Journal of Social and Personal Relationships*, *38*(7), 1987-2007

Parija, A. C. P. P. (2021). The Love-Breakup study: Defining love and exploring reasons for the breakup of romantic relationships. *Journal of Health Sexuality and Culture*, *7*(2), 41-48.

Park, Y. Debrot, A., Spielmann, S. S., Joel, S., Impett, E., & MacDonald, G. (2019).Distinguishing dismissing from fearful attachment in the association between closeness and commitment. *Social Psychological and Personality Science*, *10*(4), 563-572.

Park, Y., Impett, E. A., Spielmann, S. S., Joel, S., & MacDonald, G. (2021). Lack of intimacy prospectively predicts breakup. *Social Psychological and Personality Science*, *12*(4), 442-451.

Pattemore, C. (n.d.). *Breadcrumbing: Why you're being led on in dating.* Psych Central. https://psychcentral.com/relationships/breadcrumbing#what-to-do

Peterson, K. K. (2014). Distance Makes the Heart Grow Fonder: Do Long-Distance Relationships Have an Effect on Levels of Intimacy in Romantic Relationships?*Global Tides*, *8*(1), 8.

Pham, M. N., & Shackelford, T. K. (2013).Oral sex as mate retention behaviour. *Personality and Individual Differences*, *55*(2), 185-188.

Pincus, A. L., & Lukowitsky, M. R. (2010).Pathological narcissism and narcissistic personality disorder. *Annual review of clinical psychology*, *6*, 421-446.

Popova, M. (2021, November 29). *Love and Limerence: The forgotten psychologist Dorothy Tennov's revelatory research into the confusions of bonding.* The Marginalian. https://www.themarginalian.org/2021/11/25/love-and-limerence-dorothy-tennov/

Portmann, J. (2017). Chatting is not cheating. *The philosophy of sex: Contemporary readings*, 85-102.

Previti, D., & Amato, P. R.(2004). Is infidelity a cause or a consequence of poor marital quality? *Journal of Social and Personal Relationships*, *21*(2), 217-230.

Prins, K. S.,Buunk, B. P., & VanYperen, N. W. (1993).Equity, normative disapproval and extramarital relationships. *Journal of Social and Personal relationships*, *10*(1), 39-53.

Quoidbach, J.,Wood, A. M., & Hansenne, M. (2009). Back to the future: The effect of daily practice of mental time travel into the future on happiness and anxiety. *The journal of positive psychology*, *4*(5), 349-355.

Regan, P. C. (1998). Of lust and love: Beliefs about the role of sexual desire in romantic relationships. *Personal Relationships*, *5*(2), 139-157.

Regan, P. C. CITATION: Regan, PC (2000). Love relationships. In LT Szuchman & F. Muscarella(Eds.), Psychological perspectives on human sexuality (pp. 232-282). New York: John Wiley & Sons, Inc.

Regan, P. C.,&Joshi, A. (2003).Ideal partner preferences among adolescents. *Social Behaviour and Personality: an international journal*, *31*(1), 13-20.

Regan, P. C., Levin, L., Sprecher, S., Christopher, F. S., & Gate, R. (2000). Partner preferences: What characteristics do men and women desire in their short-term sexual and long-term romantic partners?.

Journal of Psychology & Human Sexuality, *12*(3), 1-21.

Rhoades,G. K., Kamp Dush, C. M., Atkins, D. C., Stanley, S. M., & Markman, H. J. (2011). Breaking up is hard to do: the impact of unmarried relationship dissolution on mental health and life satisfaction. *Journal of family psychology*, *25*(3), 366.

Ritchie,M. B., & Forth, A. E. (2016). Without concern: Predicting personal-moral transgressions from psychopathy and gender. *Personality and Individual Differences*, *94*, 247-252.

Robertson, E. L.,Walker, T. M., & Frick, P. J. (2020). Intimate partner violence perpetration and psychopathy: A comprehensive review.*European Psychologist.*

Robles, T. F.(2014). Marital quality and health: Implications for marriage in the 21st century. *Current directions in psychological science*, *23*(6), 427-432.

Rodríguez-García, M. C.,Márquez-Hernández, V. V., Granados-Gámez, G., Aguilera-Manrique, G., Martínez-Puertas, H., & Gutiérrez-Puertas, L. (2020). Development and validation of breadcrumbing in affective-sexual relationships (BREAD-ASR) questionnaire: introducing a New Online dating perpetration. *International journal of environmental research and public health*, *17*(24), 9548.

Rokach, A., &Chan, S. H. (2023). Love and infidelity: Causes and consequences. *International journal of environmental research and public health*, *20*(5), 3904.

Roman, D. (2020). Justifications of internet infidelity in Romanian women with extra-dyadic affairs: a qualitative study proposal. *New trends in psychology*, *2*(1).

Rosaline, S., & Kasaraneni, H.(2024). Surge in Extramarital Affairs During Work from Home: What We Know So far. *The Family Journal*, *32*(1), 95-101.

Rusbult, C. E. (1980). Commitment and satisfaction in romantic associations: A test of the investment model. *Journal of experimental social psychology*, *16*(2), 172-186.

Rusbult,C. E., Agnew, C., & Arriaga, X. (2011).The investment model of commitment processes. *Department of Psychological Sciences Faculty Publications*, *26*.

Rusbult, C. E., Olsen, N., Davis, J. L., & Hannon, P. A. (2001).Commitment and relationship maintenance mechanisms. In *Close romantic relationships* (pp. 95-122).Psychology Press.

Russell, V. M., Baker, L. R., & McNulty, J. K. (2013). Attachment insecurity and infidelity in marriage: Do studies of dating relationships really inform us about marriage? *Journal of Family Psychology*, *27*(2), 242.

Sakman, E., Urganci, B., & Sevi, B. (2021). Your cheating heart is just afraid of ending up alone: Fear of being single mediates the relationship between attachment anxiety and infidelity. *Personality and Individual Differences*, *168*, 110366.

Salavati, S., & Boon, S. D. (2024). The relative importance of contextual factors in judging mundane extra dyadic behaviours as infidelity: A policy-capturing study. *Personal Relationships*.

Schimmenti, A., & Bifulco, A. (2015).Linking lack of care in childhood to anxiety disorders in emerging adulthood: the role of attachment styles. *Child and Adolescent Mental Health*, *20*(1), 41-48.

Schmitt, D. P., & Jonason, P. K. (2015). Attachment and sexual permissiveness: Exploring differential associations across sexes, cultures, and facets of short-term mating. *Journal of Cross-Cultural Psychology*, *46*(1), 119-133.

Schwartz, P., & Young, L. (2009).Sexual satisfaction in committed relationships. *Sexuality Research & Social Policy*, *6*, 1-17.

Seidman, G. (2016). Narcissism, intrinsic and extrinsic romantic ideals, and relationship satisfaction. *Journal of Social and Personal Relationships*, *33*(8), 1018-1030.

Sela, Y., Shackelford, T. K., Pham, M. N., & Zeigler-Hill, V.(2015). Women's mate retention behaviours, personality traits, and fellatio. *Personality and Individual Differences*, *85*, 187-191.

Selterman, D., Garcia, J. R., & Tsapelas, I.(2019). Motivations for extradyadic infidelity revisited. *The Journal of Sex Research*, *56*(3), 273-286.

Selterman, D., Garcia, J. R., & Tsapelas, I. (2021). What do people do, say, and feel when they have affairs? Associations between extradyadic infidelity motives with behavioural, emotional, and sexual outcomes. *Journal of Sex & Marital Therapy*, *47*(3), 238-252.

Selterman, D., Joel, S., & Dale, V. (2023).No Remorse: Sexual Infidelity Is Not Clearly Linked with Relationship Satisfaction or Well-Being in Ashley Madison Users. *Archives of sexual behaviour*, 1-13.

Settersten Jr, R. A., Ottusch, T. M., & Schneider, B. (2015).Becoming adult: Meanings of markers to adulthood. *Emerging trends in the social and behavioural sciences: An interdisciplinary, searchable, and linkable resource*, 1-16.

Sevi, B., Urganci, B., & Sakman, E.(2020). Who cheats? An examination of light and dark personality traits as predictors of infidelity. *Personality and Individual Differences*, *164*, 110126.

Shackelford, T. K., Goetz, A. T., Buss, D. M., Euler, H. A., & Hoier, S. (2005). When we hurt the ones we love: Predicting violence against women from men's mate retention. *Personal Relationships*, *12*(4), 447-463.

Sharpsteen, D.J., & Kirkpatrick, L. A. (1997).Romantic jealousy and adult romantic attachment. *Journal of personality and social psychology*, *72*(3), 627.

Shaver, P. R.,& Mikulincer, M. (2007).Adult attachment strategies and the regulation of emotion. *Handbook of emotion regulation*, *446*, 465.

Shaw Taylor, L., Fiore, A. T., Mendelsohn, G. A., & Cheshire, C. (2011). "Out of my league": A real-world test of the matching hypothesis. *Personality and Social Psychology Bulletin*, *37*(7), 942-954.

Slotter, E. B., Gardner, W. L., & Finkel, E. J. (2010). Who am I without you? The influence of romantic breakup on the self-concept. *Personality and social psychology bulletin*, *36*(2), 147-160.

Sonali Singh, S. S., Shweta Pal, S. P., & Neelma Kunwar, N. K. (2009).Advantages of extra-marital relationshipsin the Indian community.

Spanier, G. B., & Margolis, R. L.(1983).Marital separation and extramarital sexual behaviour. *Journal of Sex Research*, *19*(1), 23-48.

Spielmann, S. S., MacDonald, G., Joel, S., & Impett, E. A. (2016).Longing for ex-partners out of fear of being single. *Journal of personality*, *84*(6), 799-808.

Spielmann, S. S.,MacDonald, G., Maxwell, J. A., Joel, S.,

Peragine, D., Muise, A., & Impett, E. A. (2013).Settling for less out of fear of being single. *Journal of personality and social psychology*, *105*(6), 1049.

Spielmann, S. S., MacDonald, G., Maxwell, J. A., Joel, S., Peragine, D., Muise, A., & Impett, E. A. (2013).Settling for less out of fear of being single. *Journal of personality and social psychology*, *105*(6), 1049.

Sprecher, S.(1992). How men and women expect to feel and behave in response to inequity in close relationships. *Social Psychology Quarterly*, 57-69.

Sprecher, S., & Cate, R. M. (2004).Sexual satisfaction and sexual expression as predictors of relationship satisfaction and stability. In *The handbook of sexuality in close relationships* (pp. 245-266).Psychology Press.

Sprecher, S., & Felmlee, D. (2021).Social network pressure on women and men to enter a romantic relationship and fear of being single. *Interpersona: An International Journal on Personal Relationships*, *15*(2), 246-261

Sprecher, S., Felmlee, D., Metts, S., Fehr, B., & Vanni, D. (1998). Factors associated with distress following the breakup of a close relationship. *Journal of Social and Personal Relationships*, *15*(6), 791-809.

Stafford, L.,& Canary, D. J. (1991).Maintenance strategies and romantic relationship type, gender and relational characteristics. *Journal of Social and Personal relationships*, *8*(2), 217-242.

Stafford, L., & Merolla, A. J.(2007).Idealization, reunions, and stability in long-distance dating relationships. *Journal of Social and Personal Relationships*, *24*(1), 37-54.

Stafford, L.,&Merolla, A. J. (2007).Idealization, reunions, and stability in long-distance dating relationships. *Journal of Social and Personal Relationships*, *24*(1), 37-54.

Stafford, L., Merolla, A. J., & Castle, J. D. (2006).When long-distance dating partners become geographically close. *Journal of social and personal relationships*, *23*(6), 901-919.

Stasko, E. C., & Geller, P. A. (2015, August).Reframing sexting as a positive relationship behaviour. In *123rd American Psychological Association Annual Convention, Toronto, Ontario, Canada, August 6-9, 2015.*

Sternberg, R. J. (1986).A triangular theory of love. *Psychological review*, *93*(2), 119.

Stewart, M. C., Dainton, M., &Goodboy, A. K. (2014). Maintaining relationships on Facebook: Associations with uncertainty, jealousy, and satisfaction. *Communication Reports*, *27*(1), 13-26.

Stieger, S., Preyss, A. V.,& Voracek, M. (2012).Romantic jealousy and implicit and explicit self-esteem. *Personality and Individual Differences*, *52*(1), 51-55.

Stoeber, J. (2012). Dyadic perfectionism in romantic relationships: Predicting relationship satisfaction and long term commitment. *Personality and Individual Differences*, *53*(3), 300-305.

Strachman, A., & Gable, S. L. (2006).Approach and avoidance relationship commitment. *Motivation and Emotion*, *30*, 117-126.

Strutzenberg, C. (2016). Love-bombing: a narcissistic approach to relationship formation.

Suwinyattichaiporn, T., Fontana, J., Shaknitz, L., & Linder, K. (2017). Maintaining long distance romantic relationships: The college students perspective. *Kentucky Journal of Communication*, *36*(1), 67-89.

Tashiro, T. Y., & Frazier, P.(2003). "I'll never be in a relationship like that again": Personal growth following romantic relationship breakups. *Personal relationships*, *10*(1), 113-128.

Tennov, D. (1998). *Love and limerence: The experience of being in love*. Scarborough House.

Thibaut, J. W. & Kelley, H. H. (1959).The social psychology of groups. NY: John Wiley & Sons.

Timmermans, E., Coenen, L.,& Van den Bulck, J. (2019). The Bridget Jones effect: The relationship between exposure to romantic media contents and fear of being single among emerging adults. *Psychology of Popular Media Culture*, *8*(2), 159.

Tomasoa, A. R., & Wulandari, P. Y. (2024). The Role of Avoidant Attachment and Anxious Attachment in Romantic Jealousy Among Young Adults in Long-Distance Relationships. *Jurnal Syntax Fusion*, *4*(02), 23-33.

Trub, L.,& Starks, T. J. (2017). Insecure attachments: Attachment, emotional regulation, sexting and condomless sex among women in relationships. *Computers in Human Behaviour*, *71*, 140-147.

Tsapelas, I. (2011). *Self-expansion as a predictor of attention to alternative romantic partners* (Doctoral dissertation, State University of New York at Stony Brook).

Van der Watt, A. S. J., Kidd, M., Roos, A., Lesch, E., & Seedat, S. (2023). Romantic relationship dissolutions are significantly associated with posttraumatic stress symptoms as compared to a DSM-5 Criterion event: a case-case–control comparison. *European Journal of Psychotraumatology*, *14*(2),2238585.

Van Ouytsel, J., Walrave, M., & Van Gool, E. (2014). Sexting: Between thrill and fear—How schools can respond. *The Clearing House: A Journal of Educational Strategies, Issues and Ideas*, *87*(5), 204-212.

Vanden Abeele, M., Campbell, S. W., Eggermont, S., & Roe, K. (2014). Sexting, mobile porn use, and peer group dynamics: Boys' and girls' self-perceived popularity, need for popularity, and perceived peer pressure. *Media Psychology*, *17*(1), 6-33.

Viejo, C., Ortega-Ruiz, R., & Sánchez, V. (2015). Adolescent love and well-being: The role of dating relationships for psychological adjustment. *Journal of Youth Studies*, *18*(9), 1219-1236.

Vittengl, J. R.,& Holt, C. S. (2000).Getting acquainted: The relationship of self-disclosure and social attraction to positive affect. *Journal of Social and Personal Relationships*, *17*(1), 53-66.

Wachs, S., Wright, M. F., Gámez-Guadix, M., & Döring, N. (2021). How are consensual, non-consensual, and pressured sexting linked to depression and self-harm?The moderating effects of demographic variables. *International journal of environmental research and public health*, *18*(5), 2597.

Wakin, A. H., & Vo, D. B. (2008). Love-variant: The Wakin-Vo IDR model of limerence.

Wei, M., Russell, D. W.,Mallinckrodt, B., & Vogel, D. L. (2007). The Experiences in Close Relationship Scale (ECR)-short form: Reliability, validity, and factor structure. *Journal of personality assessment*, *88*(2), 187-204.

Weiser, D. A.,& Weigel, D. J. (2016). Self-efficacy in romantic relationships: direct and indirect effects on relationship maintenance and satisfaction. *Personality and Individual Differences*, *89*, 152-156.

Weisskirch, R.S., Drouin, M., & Delevi, R.(2017).Relational

anxiety and sexting. *The Journal of Sex Research*, *54*(6), 685-693.

Wesche, R., Claxton, S. E., Lefkowitz, E. S., & van Dulmen, M. H. (2018). Evaluations and future plans after casual sexual experiences: Differences across partner type. *The Journal of Sex Research*, *55*(9), 1180-1191.

Whisman, M.A., Gordon, K.C., & Chatav, Y. (2007).Predicting sexual infidelity in a population-based sample of married individuals. *Journal of family psychology*, *21*(2), 320.

Whitty, M. T., & Quigley, L.L.(2008).Emotional and sexual infidelity offline and in cyberspace. *Journal of Marital and Family Therapy*, *34*(4), 461-468.

Why and how we fall victim to Breadcrumbers. (n.d.). Psychology Today. https://www.psychologytoday.com/us/blog/love-digitally/202311/why-and-how-we-fall-victim-to-breadcrumbers

Wiederman, M. W. & Hurd, C. (1999). Extradyadic involvement during dating. *Journal of Social and Personal Relationships*, *16*(2), 265-274.

Wiggins, J.D., & Lederer, D.A. (1984).Differential antecedents of infidelity in marriage.*American Mental Health Counselors Association Journal.*

Willmott, L., & Bentley, E. (2014). *Love and limerence: Harness the limbic brain.* Lathbury House Limited.

Willmott, L., & Bentley, E. (2015).Exploring the lived-Experience of limerence: A Journey toward authenticity. *The Qualitative Report*, *20*(1), 20-38.

Wolf, N. R. (2017). *Investigating limerence: Predictors of limerence, measure validation, and goal progress* (Doctoral dissertation, University of Maryland, College Park)

Woolard, A. (2011). The frequency, attitudes, and beliefs of sexting among college students

Woollard, F. (2010).Cheating with Jenna: monogamy, pornography and erotica.

Wurst, S., Humberg, S., & Back, M. (2018). Preprint of" Rose-ColorColoured Glasses in Initial Romantic Encounters? Examining Positive Partner Illusions and Their Interpersonal Consequences in the Very Early Stages of Romantic Acquaintance".

Zgaga, S., & Avsec, A.(2012). Relationship termination in emerging adulthood: Coping strategies as predictors of posttraumatic growth. *Psihološka obzorja*, *21*(2), 29–40. https://doi.org/10.20419/2012.21.361

9 788197 244766

Printed at Repro India Ltd.